Anonymous

S. Mary's hymnal

A collection of hymns, songs and carols for use at the Holy Eucharist, children's services, guild meetings, mission services

Anonymous

S. Mary's hymnal
A collection of hymns, songs and carols for use at the Holy Eucharist, children's services, guild meetings, mission services

ISBN/EAN: 9783337265137

Printed in Europe, USA, Canada, Australia, Japan

Cover: Foto ©Lupo / pixelio.de

More available books at **www.hansebooks.com**

THE HOLY EUCHARIST.

When you get to your seat, kneel down quietly, and say this Prayer.

Take away, O LORD, our sins, and keep us from wandering thoughts, that we may worship Thee with pure hearts and minds, through JESUS CHRIST our LORD. Amen.

PROCESSIONAL HYMN.

A

When there is no processional hymn, go to your place quietly, kneel down, while the Priest says his prayer.

Then listen while the priest begins the service.

OUR FATHER, Who art in Heaven, Hallowed be Thy Name. Thy kingdom come. Thy will be done on earth, As it is in Heaven. Give us this day our daily bread. And forgive us our trespasses, As we forgive those who trespass against us. And lead us not into temptation; But deliver us from evil. Amen.

THE COLLECT.

ALMIGHTY GOD, unto Whom all hearts are open, all desires known, and from Whom no secrets are hid: Cleanse the thoughts of our hearts by the inspiration of Thy HOLY SPIRIT, that we may perfectly love Thee, and worthily magnify Thy holy Name; through CHRIST our LORD.

AMEN.

THE TEN COMMANDMENTS.

Respond reverently after each Commandment.

People. LORD have mercy upon us and incline our hearts to keep this law.

After the last Commandment.

People. LORD have mercy upon us and write all these Thy laws in our hearts, we beseech Thee.

Sometimes the Commandments are omitted, and the Priest says instead:—

Hear what our LORD JESUS CHRIST saith. THOU shalt love the LORD thy GOD with all thy heart, and with all thy soul, and with all thy mind. This is the first and great commandment. And the second is like unto it: Thou shalt love thy neighbor as thyself. On these two commandments hang all the Law and the Prophets.

Let us pray.

O ALMIGHTY LORD, and everlasting GOD, vouchsafe, we beseech Thee, to direct, sanctify, and govern both our hearts and bodies, in the ways of Thy laws, and in the works of Thy commandments; that through Thy most mighty protection both here and ever, we may be preserved in body and soul; through our LORD and SAVIOUR JESUS CHRIST.

AMEN.

THE COLLECT FOR THE DAY.

AMEN.

THE EPISTLE.

Sit down and listen reverently.

HYMN.

(B)

THE GOSPEL.

Stand when the Gospel is given out.

Before the Gospel say:

Glory be to Thee, O LORD.

After the Gospel say:

Praise be to Thee, O CHRIST.

THE NICENE CREED.

Be careful to say this from beginning to end with the Priest.

Kneel reverently at the words in capital letters, to honour our LORD, who humbled Himself to take our nature upon Him.

Sign yourself with the Sign of the Cross, in token of your faith in CHRIST crucified, and that you are not ashamed of Him and of His Cross.

I BELIEVE in one GOD, the FATHER Almighty, Maker of Heaven and earth, And of all things visible and invisible;
And in one LORD JESUS CHRIST, the only-begotten SON of GOD, Begotten of His FATHER before all worlds, GOD of GOD, Light of Light, Very GOD of very GOD; Begotten, not made; Being of one substance with the FATHER; By Whom all things were made; Who for us men, and for our salvation came down from Heaven, AND WAS INCARNATE BY THE HOLY GHOST OF THE VIRGIN MARY, AND WAS MADE MAN: And was crucified also for us under Pontius Pilate; He suffered and was buried; And the third day He rose again according to the Scriptures; And ascended into Heaven, And sitteth on the right hand of the FATHER. And he shall come again with glory to judge both the quick and the dead: Whose kingdom shall have no end.
And I believe in the HOLY GHOST, the LORD and Giver of Life, Who proceedeth from the FATHER and the SON, Who with the FATHER and the SON together is worshipped and glorified, Who spake by the Prophets. And I believe one Catholic and Apostolic Church; I acknowledge one Baptism for the remission of sins: And I look for the Resurrection of the dead: ✠ And the Life of the world to come.   AMEN.

When there is a Sermon it follows here. Sit very still and look at the Preacher.

THE OFFERTORY SENTENCE.

Let your light so shine before men that they may see your good works, and glorify your FATHER Which is in Heaven.

HYMN.
(C)

The collection is here made. Give as often and as much as you can, and always gladly.

The Priest having read the Offertory Sentence, uncovers the Chalice or Cup, and taking in his hand the Paten, or little plate, goes to the side of the Altar and places on it sufficient Bread. Returning to the centre he offers it to GOD. Going to the side again, he takes the Wine and pours it into the Chalice, mixing with it a little water, in remembrance of the Blood and Water which issued from the SAVIOUR'S Side.

After this, he returns and offers the Chalice, calling on the HOLY SPIRIT to sanctify the offering.

After the hymn is sung kneel down.

THE PRIEST. Let us pray for the whole state of CHRIST'S Church militant.

ALMIGHTY and ever-living GOD, Who by Thy holy Apostle hast taught us to make prayers, and supplications, and to give thanks for all men: We humbly beseech Thee most mercifully to accept our alms and oblations, and to receive these our prayers, which we offer unto Thy Divine Majesty; beseeching Thee to inspire continually the Universal Church with the spirit of truth, unity and concord; And grant that all those who do confess Thy holy Name may agree in the truth of Thy holy Word, and live in unity, and godly love. We beseech Thee, also, so to direct and dispose the hearts of all Christian Rulers, that they may truly and impartially administer justice, to the punishment of wickedness and vice, and to the maintenance of Thy true religion, and virtue. Give grace, O heavenly FATHER, to all Bishops and other Ministers, that they may, both by their life and doctrine, set forth Thy true and lively Word, and rightly and duly administer Thy holy Sacraments. And to all Thy people give Thy heavenly grace; and especially to this congregation here present; that, with meek heart and due reverence, they may hear, and receive Thy holy Word; truly serving Thee in holiness and righteousness all the days of their life. And we most humbly beseech Thee, of Thy goodness, O LORD, to comfort and succour all those who, in this transitory life, are in trouble, sorrow, need, sickness, or any other adversity. And we also bless Thy holy Name for all Thy servants departed this life in Thy faith and fear; beseeching Thee to give us grace, so to follow their good examples, that with them we may be partakers of Thy heavenly kingdom. Grant this, O FATHER, for JESUS CHRIST'S sake, our only Mediator and Advocate.

AMEN.

THE SHORT EXHORTATION.

Then shall the Priest say to those who come to receive the Holy Communion:

YE who do truly and earnestly repent you of your sins, and are in love and charity with your neighbors, and intend to lead a new life, following the commandments of GOD, and walking from henceforth in His holy ways; Draw near with faith, and take this holy Sacrament to your comfort; and make your humble confession to ALMIGHTY GOD, devoutly kneeling.

Be careful to say this reverently with the Priest, sentence by sentence.

THE CONFESSION.

ALMIGHTY GOD, FATHER of our LORD JESUS CHRIST, Maker of all things, Judge of all men; We acknowledge and bewail our manifold sins and wickedness, Which we, from time to time most grievously have committed, By thought, word, and deed,

Against Thy Divine Majesty, Provoking most justly Thy wrath and indignation against us. We do earnestly repent, And are heartily sorry for these our misdoings; The remembrance of them is grievous unto us; The burden of them is intolerable. Have mercy upon us, Have mercy upon us, most merciful FATHER; for Thy SON our LORD JESUS CHRIST'S sake, Forgive us all that is past; And grant that we may ever hereafter serve and please Thee In newness of life, To the honour and glory of Thy Name; Through JESUS CHRIST our LORD. Amen.

THE ABSOLUTION.

ALMIGHTY GOD, our heavenly FATHER, who of His great mercy hath promised forgiveness of sins to all those who with hearty repentance and true faith turn unto Him; Have mercy upon you; pardon and deliver you from all your sins; confirm and strengthen you in all goodness; and bring you to everlasting life; through JESUS CHRIST our LORD.

AMEN.

THE COMFORTABLE WORDS.

Hear what comfortable words our SAVIOUR CHRIST saith unto all who truly turn to Him:—

COME unto Me, all ye that travail and are heavy laden, and I will refresh you. St. Matt. xi. 28.

So GOD loved the world, that He gave His only-begotten SON, to the end that all that believe in Him, should not perish, but have everlasting life. St. John iii., 16.

Hear also what Saint Paul saith:—

This is a true saying, and worthy of all men to be received, That CHRIST JESUS came into the world to save sinners. I. Tim. i., 15.

Hear also what Saint John saith:—

If any man sin, we have an Advocate with the FATHER, JESUS CHRIST the righteous; and He is the Propitiation for our sins. 1 St. John ii. 1, 2.

THE SURSUM CORDA.

PRIEST. Lift up your hearts.

Answer. We lift them up unto the LORD.

PRIEST. Let us give thanks unto our LORD GOD.

Answer. It is meet and right so to do.

The Priest says the Preface. It is so called because it leads up to the more solemn part of the service.

(Sometimes there is a special Preface to be found in the Prayer-Book.)

THE PREFACE.

IT is very meet, right, and our bounden duty, that we should at all times, and in all places, give thanks unto Thee, O LORD, Holy FATHER, Almighty, Everlasting God.

THEREFORE with Angels and Archangels, and with all the company of Heaven, we laud and magnify Thy glorious Name; evermore praising Thee, and saying:—

After this the Sanctus, in which join with head bowed down, thinking how even the Holy Angels dare not look on the Holiness of GOD, but veil their faces, and bow before Him.

THE SANCTUS.

Holy, Holy, Holy, LORD GOD of Hosts, Heaven and earth are full of Thy glory; Glory be to Thee, O LORD Most High.

AMEN.

THE PRAYER OF HUMBLE ACCESS.

WE do not presume to come to this Thy Table, O merciful LORD, trusting in our own righteousness, but in Thy manifold and great mercies. We are not worthy so much as to gather up the crumbs under Thy Table. But Thou art the same LORD, whose property is always to have mercy; Grant us, therefore, gracious LORD, so to eat the flesh of Thy dear SON, JESUS CHRIST, and to drink His blood, that our sinful bodies may be made clean by His body, and our souls washed through His most precious blood, and that we may evermore dwell in Him and He in us.

THE BENEDICTUS,

Blessed is He that cometh in the Name of the LORD. Hosanna in the Highest.

Kneel very reverently and keep quite still. It is better to keep the eyes shut, and bow the head.

THE PRAYER OF CONSECRATION.

ALL glory be to Thee, Almighty GOD, our heavenly FATHER, for that Thou, of Thy tender mercy, didst give Thine only SON Jesus CHRIST to suffer death upon the Cross for our redemption; Who made there (by His one oblation of Himself once offered) a full, perfect and sufficient sacrifice, oblation, and satisfaction, for the sins of the whole world; and did institute, and in His holy Gospel command us to continue, a perpetual memory of that His precious death and sacrifice, until His coming again: For in the night in which He was betrayed, He took Bread; and when He had given thanks He brake it, and gave it to His disciples, saying, "TAKE, EAT, THIS IS MY BODY, WHICH IS GIVEN FOR YOU; DO THIS IN REMEMBRANCE OF ME." Likewise, after supper, He took the Cup: and when He had given thanks, He gave it to them, saying, "DRINK YE ALL OF THIS, FOR THIS IS MY BLOOD OF THE NEW TESTAMENT, WHICH IS SHED FOR YOU, AND FOR MANY, FOR THE REMISSION OF SINS; DO THIS, AS OFT AS YE SHALL DRINK IT, IN REMEMBRANCE OF ME."

Wherefore, O LORD and heavenly FATHER, according to the institution of Thy dearly beloved SON our SAVIOUR JESUS CHRIST, we, Thy humble servants, do celebrate and make here before Thy Divine Majesty, with these Thy Holy Gifts, which we now offer unto Thee, the Memorial Thy SON hath commanded us to make: having in remembrance His blessed passion and precious death, His mighty resurrection and glorious ascension; rendering unto Thee most hearty thanks for the innumerable benefits procured unto us by the same. And we most humbly beseech Thee, O merciful Father, to hear us; and, of Thy almighty goodness, vouchsafe to bless and sanctify, with Thy WORD and HOLY SPIRIT, these Thy gifts and creatures of bread and wine; that we, receiving them according Thy SON our SAVIOUR JESUS CHRIST'S holy institution, in remembrance of His death and passion, may be partakers of His most blessed Body and Blood. And we earnestly desire Thy fatherly goodness, mercifully to accept this our Sacrifice of praise and thanksgiving; most humbly beseeching Thee to grant, that by the merits and death of Thy SON JESUS CHRIST, and through faith in His Blood, we, and all Thy whole Church, may obtain remission of our sins, and all other benefits of His Passion. And here we offer and present unto Thee, O LORD, ourselves, our souls and bodies, to be a reasonable, holy, and living sacrifice unto Thee; humbly beseeching Thee, that we, and all others who shall be partakers of this Holy Communion, may worthily receive the most precious Body and Blood of Thy SON JESUS CHRIST, be filled with Thy grace and heavenly benediction, and made one body with Him, that He may dwell in them, and they in Him. And although we are unworthy, through our manifold sins, to offer unto Thee any sacrifice, yet we beseech Thee to accept this our bounden duty and service; not weighing our merits, but pardoning our offences, through JESUS CHRIST our LORD; by Whom, and with Whom, in the unity of the HOLY GHOST, all honour and glory be unto Thee, O FATHER Almighty, world without end.

AMEN.

Say softly:—

Most precious FATHER, accept this Holy Sacrifice at the hands of Thy Priest, in union with that All-Holy Sacrifice which Thy beloved SON, through His whole life, at the Last Supper, and upon the Cross, offered unto Thee for me and for all. Amen.

THE AGNUS DEI.

O LAMB of GOD, that takest away the sins of the world, have mercy upon us.

O Lamb of God, that takest away the sins of the world, have mercy upon us.

O Lamb of God, that takest away the sins of the world, grant us Thy peace.

HYMN.
(D)

[If you are going to receive the Holy Communion, go up quietly when others go, and kneel at the Altar-rail.

When the Priest brings you the Holy Sacrament, say softly:—

Lord, I am not worthy that Thou shouldst come under my roof, but speak the word only, and my soul shall be healed.

After you have received, say softly:

Thanks be to Thee, O God, for this unspeakable gift!

Then return gently to your place in Church, and kneel down.

You will find other prayers and devotions in your own private book of prayers.]

Those who do not communicate must be careful not to look about. Join in the hymn, if one is being sung. If the hymn is finished, kneel quietly, and think of the LORD JESUS present, and looking down in love on His children.

THE LORD'S PRAYER.

Say this carefully all through with the Priest.

Our Father, Who art in Heaven, Hallowed be Thy Name. Thy kingdom come. Thy will be done on earth, As it is in

Heaven. Give us this day our daily bread. And forgive us our trespasses, As we forgive those who trespass against us. And lead us not into temptation; But deliver us from evil: For Thine is the kingdom, and the power, and the glory, for ever and ever. Amen.

THE POST-COMMUNION.

ALMIGHTY and ever-living GOD, we most heartily thank Thee, for that Thou dost vouchsafe to feed us, who have duly received these holy mysteries, with the spiritual food of the most precious Body and Blood of Thy SON our SAVIOUR JESUS CHRIST; and dost assure us thereby of Thy favor and goodness toward us; and that we are very members incorporate in the mystical Body of Thy SON, which is the blessed company of all faithful people; and are also heirs through hope of Thy everlasting kingdom, by the merits of the most precious death and passion of Thy dear SON. And we most humbly beseech Thee, O heavenly FATHER, so to assist us with Thy grace, that we may continue in that holy fellowship, and do all such good works as Thou hast prepared for us to walk in: through JESUS CHRIST our LORD, to Whom, with Thee and the HOLY GHOST, be all honour and glory, world without end.

AMEN.

THE GLORIA IN EXCELSIS

When this is sung stand up and join in it heartily

Glory be to GOD on high, and on earth peace, good-will towards men. We praise Thee, we bless Thee, we worship Thee, we glorify Thee, we give thanks to Thee, for Thy great glory, O LORD GOD, heavenly KING, GOD the FATHER Almighty.

O LORD, the only begotten SON, JESUS CHRIST; O LORD GOD, LAMB of GOD, SON of the FATHER, that takest away the sins of the world, have mercy upon us. Thou that takest away the sins of the world, have mercy upon us. Thou that takest away the sins of the world, receive our prayer. Thou that sittest at the right hand of GOD the FATHER, have mercy upon us.

For Thou only art holy; Thou only art the LORD; Thou only, O CHRIST, with the HOLY GHOST, art most high in the glory of GOD the FATHER. Amen.

OR HYMN.

(E)

THE BLESSING.

THE peace of GOD which passeth all understanding, keep your hearts and minds in the knowledge and love of GOD, and of His SON JESUS CHRIST our LORD. And the blessing of GOD Almighty, the FATHER, ✠ the SON, and the HOLY GHOST, be amongst you, and remain with you always.

AMEN.

Say softly to yourself :

I BESEECH Thee, O LORD JESUS CHRIST, that Thy passion may be unto me virtue, whereby I may be fenced, protected and defended. Let the sprinkling of Thy Blood be to me the washing away of all my sins. Let Thy Death be to me everlasting glory, both now and forever. Amen.

During the Ablutions begin the

PROCESSIONAL HYMN.

(F)

Stand up when the Priest leaves the Altar, and stand very still. After the Priest has gone into the Sacristy, then kneel down and say this prayer silently :—

BLESSED be Thy Name, O LORD GOD, for that it hath pleased Thee to have Thy habitation among the sons of men, and to dwell in the midst of the assembly of the saints upon the earth; bless, we beseech Thee the service of this day, and grant that in this place Thy holy Name may be worshipped in truth and purity through all generations, through JESUS CHRIST our LORD. Amen.

Go quietly and reverently out of Church.

LITTLE EVENSONG.

¶ *When all are in their places, the Officiant may begin by saying one of the sentences suited to the Church Season, from the Book of Common Prayer, after which all shall kneel and say:*

OUR FATHER.

O LORD, open Thou our lips.

And our mouth shall show forth Thy praise.

¶ *Here, all standing up, the Officiant shall say,*

Glory be to the FATHER, and to the SON, and to the HOLY GHOST.

As it was in the beginning, is now and ever shall be, world without end. Amen.

Praise ye the LORD.

The Lord's Name be praised.

¶ *Then shall follow one or more of these Psalms, after each of which shall be said,*
Glory be.

PSALM 110. III. 2.

The **Lord** said **unto my** Lórd: Sit thou on my right hánd. until I make thine énemies thy **foot**stool.

2 The Lórd shall sénd the ród of thy pówer **out** of **Sion**: be thou rúler even in the midst **among** thine **enemies**.

3 In the dáy of thy pówer shall the people óffer thee free-will ófferings, with an **holy worship**: the déw of thy birth is of the **womb** of the **morning**.

4 The Lórd swáre. **and** will **not** repént: Thou art a Priest for éver, after the órder **of** Melchizedech.

(14)

5 The Lórd upon thy **right** hand : shall woúnd even **kings** in the **day** of his wráth.

6 He shall júdge among the heáthen, he shall fill the pláces with the **dead bodies** : and smíte in súnder the heáds over divers **countries**.

7 He shall drink of the **brook in** the way: thérefore shall **he** lift **up** his heád.

PSALM 111. VII. 1: A.

I **will** give thánks unto the **Lord** with my **whole** heart : sécretly among the faithful, and in the **congregation**.

2 The **works** of the **Lord** are greát : sought oút of all **them** that have **pleasure** therein.

3 His wórk is wórthy to be praised, and **had** in **honour** : and his ríghteousness endureth for **ever**.

4 The mérciful and grácious Lórd hath **so** done his **marvellous** wórks : that they oúght to be **had** in remembrance.

5 He hath given meát unto **them** that **fear** him : he shall éver be mindful **of** his **covenant**.

6 He hath shéwed his peóple the **power of** his works : that he may give them the héritage of the **heathen**.

7 The wórks of his hánds are **verity** and **judgment** : áll **his** commandments are true.

8 They stand fást for **ever** and **ever**: and are dóne in **truth** and equity.

9 He sént redémption **unto** his **people**: he hath commanded his cóvenant for éver, hóly and **reverend is** his Náme.

10 The feár of the Lórd is the beginning of **wisdom**: a goód understánding have all they that do thereafter, the praise of it en**dure**th forever.

PSALM 112.   IV. 1. C.

Blessed is the mán that **feareth** the **Lord**: he hath greát delight in **his** commandments.

2 His seéd shall be míghty upon **earth**: the generátion of the faithful **shall** be **blessed**.

3 Riches and plénteousness shall be **in** his **house**: and his righteousness en**dur**eth for **ever**.

4 Unto the gódly there aríseth up **light** in the **darkness**: he is mérciful, **loving** and **right**eous.

5 A goód man is **merciful** and **lendeth**: and will guide his **words** with discretion.

6 For he shall **never** be **moved**: and the ríghteous shall be hád in everlasting re**mem**brance.

7 He will not be afraíd of any **evil tidings**: for his heárt stándeth fást, and believeth **in** the Lórd.

8 His heart is stáblished and **will** not **shrink** : until he see his desire u**pon** his enemies.

9 He hath dispérsed abroad and given to the poor, and his righteousness re**maineth** for **ever**: his horn shall be exalted with **honour**.

10 The ungódly shall seé it and it shall grieve him, he shall gnásh with his teéth and con**sume** away: the desire of the un**godly** shall **perish**.

PSALM 113.   VIII. 1. A.

Praise the Lórd ye **servants**: O **praise** the **Name** of the Lórd.

2 Bléssed be the Náme of the **Lord**: from this time **forth** for evermore.

3 The Lord's Náme is **praised** : from the rising up of the sún unto the **going down** of the same.

4 The Lórd is high above áll **heathen** : and His glóry **above** the heavens.

5 Who is like unto the Lórd our Gód, that hath His dwélling so **high** : and yet húmbleth himself to behóld the things that **are** in **heaven** and eárth.

6 He táketh up the símple out of the **dust**: and lifteth the poorout of the mire.

7 That he may sét him with the **princes** : éven **with the** prínces **of** his **people**.

8 He máketh the bárren woman to keép **house** : and to be a joyful **mother** of **children**.

PSALM 114. Peregrinus A.

When **Israél cáme out** of Egypt : and the hoúse of Jácob from among the **stränge** people.

2 Júdah **was** his **sanctuary** : and Israel **his** dominion.

3 The **séa sáw** that and fléd : Jordan was **driven** báck.

4 The **mountains skípped like** ráms : and the little **hills** like **young** sheép.

5 What aileth thee **O** thou **sea** that thou **fléddest** ; and thou Jórdan, that **thou** wast **driven** báck.

6 Ye moúntains, **that** ye **skipped like** ráms : and ye little **hills** like **young** sheép.

7 Trémble thou **earth**, at the **présence of** the Lórd : at the présence of the **God** of **Jacob**.

8 Who túrned the hárd rock **into** a **standing water** : and the flint-stone **into** a **springing** wéll.

PSALM 115. Peregrinus A.

Not unto ús O Lórd, nót unto ús, but unto **Thy Name give** the praíse : for Thy lóving mércy **and** for Thy **truth's** sake.

2 **Wherefore shall** the **heathen** say : **Where** is now **their** Gód.

3 As for our **God he** is in **heaven**: he hath done whatsoever **pleased** him.

4 Their **idols** are **silver** and **gold**: even the **work** of **men's** hands.

5 **They** have **mouths** and **speak** not: eyes have **they** and **see** not.

6 **They** have **ears** and **hear** not: noses have **they** and **smell** not.

7 **They** have **hands** and **handle** not, **feet** have **they** and **walk** not: neither **speak** they **through** their throat.

8 They that **make** them are **like** unto them: and so are all such as **put** their **trust** in them.

9 But thou house of **Israel trust** thou **in** the Lord: he is their **succour and defence**.

10 Ye house of **Aaron put your trust** in the Lord: he is their **helper and defender.**

11 Ye that fear the **Lord put** your **trust** in the Lord: he is their **helper and defender**,

12 The Lord hath been mindful of **us**, and **he** shall **bless** us: even he shall bless the house of Israel, he shall bless the **house** of Aaron.

13 He shall **bless them** that **fear** the Lord: **both small** and great.

14 The **Lord** shall increase you **more** and more: **you** and your **children**.

15 **Ye** are the **blessed of** the Lórd: who **máde heaven** and eárth.

16 All the **whóle heavens are** the Lórd's: the eárth hath he given **to** the **children** of mén.

17 The **déad praise** not **thee** O Lórd: neither all they that go **down** into silence.

18 But **we** will **praise** the Lórd: from this time fórth, for evermóre **Praise** the Lórd.

PSALM 117. VI. A

O **Praise** the Lórd **all** ye **heathen**: praíse him **all** ye **nations**.

2 For his mérciful kíndness is evermóre and **more towards** us: and the trúth of the Lórd endúreth for **ever**. **Praise** the Lórd.

¶ *Then shall be read a Lesson from the Holy Scriptures.*

¶ *After which shall be sung*

THE SONG OF THE BLESSED VIRGIN MARY.

Magnificat, S. Luke i. 46.

I, III, VI or VII.

My **soul** doth **magnify** the Lórd: and my spírit hath rejoíced in **God** my Savíour.

2 **For** He **hath regarded**: the lówliness of **His** hand maiden.

3 **For** behold from **henceforth**: all generátions shall **call** me **blessed**.

4. For **He** that is mighty, hath **magnified** me: and **holy is** His Náme.

5 And His **mercy** is on **them** that **fear** Him: throughout all **generations**.

6 He hath **showed strength with** His árm: He hath scáttered the proúd, in the imagination **of** their hearts.

7 He **hath** put dówn, the **mighty from** their seát: and hath exalted the **humble** and meék.

8 He hath **filled** the **hungry** with **good** things: and the rich He hath **sent empty** away.

9 He remembering His mércy, hath hólpen His **servant Israel**: as He prómised to our fórefathers, Abraham and his **seed**. forever.

Glory be to the **Father** and **to** the Són: and **to** the **Holy Ghóst**.

As it **was** in the beginning, is nów, and **ever shall** be: wórld without end. Amen.

¶ *Then shall be said the Apostle's Creed, by Officiant and people.*

I BELIEVE.

The LORD be with you.
And with Thy Spirit.

Let us pray.

O LORD, show Thy mercy upon us.
And grant us Thy salvation.

O GOD, make clean our hearts within us.

And take not Thy Holy Spirit from us.

❡ *Then shall be said,*

THE COLLECT FOR THE DAY.

❡ *And after that the following:*

A Collect for Peace.

O GOD, from Whom all holy desires, all good counsels, and all just works do proceed: give unto Thy servants that peace, which the world cannot give: that our hearts may be set to obey Thy commandments, and also that by Thee, we, being defended from the fear of our enemies, may pass our time in rest and quietness: through the merits of JESUS CHRIST our SAVIOUR. *Amen.*

A Collect for Aid against Perils.

Lighten our darkness, we beseech Thee, O LORD; and by Thy great mercy defend us from all perils and dangers of this night; for the love of Thine only SON, our SAVIOUR, JESUS CHRIST. *Amen.*

2 *Cor.* xiii. 14.

☩ The Grace of our LORD JESUS CHRIST, and the Love of GOD, and the Fellowship of the HOLY GHOST, be with us all evermore. *Amen.*

COMMEMORATIONS.

¶ *Which may be used at discretion at the close of service.*

1. OF THE INCARNATION.

Ant. Hail, thou that art highly favoured, the LORD is with thee: blessed art thou among women.

V. Behold the handmaid of the LORD.
R. *Be it unto me according to thy word.*

LET US PRAY.

We beseech Thee, O LORD, pour Thy grace into our hearts: that as we have known the incarnation of Thy SON JESUS CHRIST by the message of an Angel, so by His cross and passion we may be brought unto the glory of His resurrection; through the same JESUS CHRIST our LORD. *Amen.*

2. OF ALL SAINTS.

Ant. I beheld, and, lo, a great multitude: which no man could number, of all nations, and kindreds, and people, and tongues, stood before the throne.

V. The Righteous shall receive a glorious Kingdom.
R. *And a beautiful crown from the Lord's Hand.*

LET US PRAY.

O Almighty GOD, who hast knit together Thine elect in one communion and fellowship, in the mystical body of Thy SON CHRIST our Lord; Grant us grace so to follow Thy blessed Saints in all virtuous and godly living, that we may come to those unspeakable joys, which Thou hast prepared for those who unfeignedly love Thee; through JESUS CHRIST our Lord. *Amen.*

3. OF THE HOLY ANGELS.

Ant. Their angels do always behold: the face of My FATHER which is in Heaven.

V. He shall give His Angels charge over thee.

R. *To keep thee in all thy ways.*

LET US PRAY.

O Everlasting GOD, Who hast ordained and constituted the services of Angels and men in a wonderful order: Mercifully grant, that as Thy holy Angels always do Thee service in Heaven, so, by Thy appointment, they may succour and defend us on earth; through JESUS CHRIST our LORD. *Amen.*

4. OF THE HOLY INNOCENTS.

Ant. These were redeemed from among men: being the first-fruits unto GOD and to the LAMB.

V. Blessed are the pure in heart.

R. *For they shall see God.*

Let us Pray.

O Almighty God, Who out of the mouths of babes and sucklings hast ordained strength, and madest infants to glorify Thee by their deaths: Mortify and kill all vices in us, and so strengthen us by Thy grace, that by the innocency of our lives, and constancy of our faith even unto death, we may glorify Thy holy Name; through Jesus Christ our Lord. *Amen.*

5. OF THE HOLY CROSS.

Ant. He humbled Himself and became obedient unto death: even the death of the Cross.

V. God forbid that I should glory.

R. *Save in the Cross of our Lord Jesus Christ.*

Let us Pray.

O Saviour of the world, Who by Thy Cross and precious Blood hast redeemed us; Save us, and help us, we humbly beseech Thee. O Lord. *Amen.*

6. OF PENITENT SINNERS.

Ant.—Behold now is the accepted time: behold now is the day of salvation.

V.—The sacrifice of God is a troubled spirit.

R. *A broken and contrite heart, O God, Thou shalt not despise.*

LET US PRAY.

O LORD, we beseech Thee mercifully hear our prayers, and spare all those who confess their sins unto Thee; that they, whose consciences by sin are accused, by Thy merciful pardon may be absolved; through CHRIST our LORD. *Amen.*

7. OF THE CHURCH.

Ant. In Him all the building fitly framed together: groweth unto a holy temple in the LORD.

V. Now therefore are we no more strangers.

R. *But of the household of God.*

LET US PRAY.

LORD, we beseech Thee to keep Thy household the Church in continual godliness; that through Thy protection it may be free from all adversities, and devoutly given to serve Thee in good works, to the glory of Thy Name; through JESUS CHRIST our LORD. *Amen.*

8. OF A HAPPY DEATH.

Ant. I heard a voice from heaven saying unto me: Write, from henceforth blessed are the dead, who die in the LORD.

V. O LORD, save Thy servants.

R. *Who put their trust in Thee.*

Let us Pray.

O God, Whose days are without end, and Whose mercies cannot be numbered; Make us, we beseech Thee, deeply sensible of the shortness and uncertainty of human life; and let Thy Holy Spirit lead us through this vale of misery, in holiness and righteousness, all the days of our lives: That, when we shall have served Thee in our generation, we may be gathered unto our fathers, having the testimony of a good conscience; in the communion of the Catholic Church; in the confidence of a certain faith; in the comfort of a reasonable, religious and holy hope: in favour with Thee our God, and in perfect charity with the world. All which we ask through Jesus Christ our Lord. *Amen.*

9. OF THE FAITHFUL DEPARTED.

Ant. I will walk before the Lord: in the land of the living.

V. For there is mercy with Thee.

R. *Therefore shalt Thou be feared.*

Let us Pray.

Almighty God, with Whom do live the spirits of those who depart hence in the Lord, and with Whom the souls of the faithful, after they are delivered from the burden of the flesh, are in joy and felicity: We give Thee hearty thanks for the good examples of all those Thy servants, who, having finished their course in faith, do now rest from their labours. And we beseech Thee, that we, with all those who are departed in the true faith of Thy holy Name, [   ] may have our perfect consummation and bliss, both in body and soul, in Thy eternal and everlasting glory: through JESUS CHRIST our LORD. *Amen.*

¶ *After the Commemorations the Officiant shall say:*

V. The LORD be with you.
R. *And with thy spirit.*

¶ *And then close with the Blessing or the following:*

Unto GOD's gracious mercy and protection we commit us. The LORD bless ✠ us, and keep us. The LORD make His Face to shine upon us, and be gracious unto us. The LORD lift up His countenance upon us, and give us peace, both now and evermore. *Amen.*

S. Mary's Hymnal

A COLLECTION OF

Hymns, Songs and Carols

FOR USE AT

The Holy Eucharist
Children's Services
Guild Meetings
Mission Services

WITH AN

Alphabetical Index

ALSO A

Full Index for Seasons and Subjects

BALTIMORE
The Sisters of S. Mary and All Saints,
409 W. Biddle Street.

Copyright, 1891,
BY W. C. CLAPP.

COMPILER'S PREFACE.

This little book is the result of an attempt to meet the actual needs of two different mission works, and, with few exceptions, the hymns here included have stood the test of use. It has been the conviction of the compiler that Catholic and Evangelical are not contradictory terms, but that each includes the other. The present collection therefore embraces hymns subjective in character as well as those expressing the glorious objective realities of the Faith.

But it should be remembered that hymns, like other poetical writings, rarely present all ides of the truth in any one composition. It is hoped, however, that each one in this book is capable of a right construction and presents a phase of the truth. The responsibility for the use of a hymn upon any particular occasion should rest, of course, with the officiant, and it is a matter for his careful consideration.

The hymns are not arranged according to subject. It is thought that the indices will give all possible and necessary aid in selection.

A person, using a hymnal constantly, soon learns the numbers.

No effort has been made to include a complete selection of carols. The demand for a succession of new ones is quite general, and could hardly be met by any other than a periodical publication.

The compiler has endeavored to avoid transgression of any copyright. He craves pardon if he has failed through ignorance in any case. He wishes to express his gratitude to the authors who have kindly granted permission to use their compositions.

Finally he would state that any profits arising from the sale of this book will be used in the mission work of the Church.

HYMNS.

1

A few more years shall roll,
  A few more seasons come,
And we shall be with those that rest
  Asleep within the tomb;
    Then, O my LORD, prepare
    My soul for that great day;
  O wash me in Thy precious Blood,
    And take my sins away.

A few more suns shall set
  O'er these dark hills of time,
And we shall be where suns are not,
  A far serener clime;
    Then, O my LORD, prepare
    My soul for that blest day;
  O wash me in Thy precious Blood,
    And take my sins away.

A few more storms shall beat
  On this wild rocky shore,
And we shall be where tempests cease,
  And surges swell no more;
    Then, O my LORD, prepare
    My soul for that calm day;
  O wash me in Thy precious Blood,
    And take my sins away.

A few more struggles here,
  A few more partings o'er,
A few more toils, a few more tears,
  And we shall weep no more;
    Then, O my LORD, prepare
    My soul for that bright day;
  O wash me in Thy precious Blood,
    And take my sins away.

'Tis but a little while
And He shall come again,
Who died that we might live, Who lives
That we with Him may reign;
Then, O my LORD, prepare
My soul for that glad day;
O wash me in Thy precious Blood,
And take my sins away.—Amen.

2

O JESU, Thou art standing
  Outside the fast-closed door,
In lowly patience waiting
  To pass the threshold o'er.
We bear the Name of Christians,
  His Name and sign we bear:
O shame, thrice shame upon us,
  To keep Him standing there.

O JESU, Thou art knocking,
  And lo, that Hand is scarr'd,
And thorns Thy Brow encircle,
  And tears Thy Face have marr'd.
O love that passeth knowledge,
  So patiently to wait!
O sin that hath no equal,
  So fast to bar the gate!

O JESU, Thou art pleading
  In accents meek and low,
"I died for you, My children,
  And will ye treat Me so?"
O LORD, with shame and sorrow
  We open now the door:
Dear Saviour, enter, enter,
  And leave us nevermore.—Amen.

3

O happy Fold! O happy Church!
   The living and the dead
Forever and forever more
   Unite in CHRIST their Head.

They have one Faith, they have one Hope
   Wherever they may be:
And death itself can never quench
   Their boundless Charity.

The glorious Saints forever blest,
   Who stand before GOD's Throne,
Will hear amidst their endless bliss,
   The feeblest infant's moan.

The nearer that they are to GOD
   The deeper burns their love;
How many helpers there have we
   In that bright world above!

And in this world of grief and care
   Each day and weary hour,
Saints are united, each helps each,
   By GOD's almighty power.

One here may work, one there may pray,
   One suffer and one rest,
But all the holy think or do
   Is joined in union blest.

O happy Fold! O blessed Church!
   If here so much is given,
O what will our communion be
   When all are safe in Heaven!

To GOD the FATHER, GOD the SON,
   And SPIRIT glory be,
As was and is and shall be so
   To all eternity.—Amen.

4

Before the Throne of GOD above
   The glorious Angels stand,
Their only wish, their only joy,
   To do their LORD's command.
Some ever rest before His Face
   And praise Him all day long,
Singing in never-ending strains
   Their blessed joyous song.

And some for GOD's dear children care
   And o'er them spread their wings,
To guard them from the tempter's snare
   And from all hurtful things.
Some Angels go beside the Priest,
   When he is called to see
The sick and dying ones, for there
   The Angels love to be.

Some stand where penitents pour out
   Their tale of sin and woe,
And joy to see the Precious Blood
   O'er the forgiven flow.
These holy Angels never choose,
   And never wish nor ask
For other work than what GOD gives
   To be their daily task.

So we must like the Angels be,
   Not choosing good nor ill,
But humbly striving day by day
   To do GOD's holy Will.
Grant LORD, that at my dying bed
   May stand my Guardian blest,
And may he bear my cleansed soul
   Safe to my endless rest.   —Amen.

5

Of the FATHER'S Love begotten
  Ere the worlds began to be,
He is Alpha and Omega,
  He the source, the ending He,
Of the things that are, that have been,
  And that future years shall see,
    Evermore and evermore!

O that Birth for ever blessed,
  When the Virgin, full of grace,
By the Holy Ghost conceiving,
  Bare the SAVIOUR of our race;
And the Babe, the world's REDEEMER,
  First revealed His sacred Face,
    Evermore and evermore!

This is He Whom seers in old time
  Chanted of with one accord;
Whom the voices of the Prophets
  Promised in their faithful word;
Now He shines, the long-expected;
  Let creation praise its LORD:
    Evermore and evermore!

O ye heights of Heaven adore Him!
  Angel-hosts, His praises sing!
All dominions, bow before Him,
  And extol our GOD and King:
Let no tongue on earth be silent,
  Every voice in concert ring,
    Evermore and evermore!

Thee let old men, Thee let young men,
  Thee let boys in chorus sing;
Matrons, virgins, little maidens,
  With glad voices answering;
Let their guileless songs re-echo,
  And the heart its praises bring,
    Evermore and evermore!

CHRIST! to Thee with GOD the FATHER,
 And, O HOLY GHOST, to Thee!
Hymn, and chant, and high thanksgiving
 And unwearied praises be,
Honor, glory and dominion,
 And eternal victory,
   Evermore and evermore!—
      Amen.

6

THREE in ONE, and ONE in THREE,
Ruler of the earth and sea,
Hear us, while we lift to Thee
  Holy chant and psalm.

Light of lights! with morning shine;
Lift on us Thy Light divine;
And let charity benign
  Breathe on us her balm.

Light of lights! when falls the even,
Let it close on sin forgiven:
Fold us in the peace of heaven,
  Shed a holy calm.

THREE in ONE, and ONE in THREE,
Dimly here we worship Thee;
With the saints hereafter we
  Hope to bear the palm. Amen.

7

When morning gilds the skies,
My heart awaking cries
  May JESUS CHRIST be praised.
Alike at work and prayer
To JESUS I repair;
  May JESUS CHRIST be praised.

When e'er the sweet church bell
Peals over hill and dell,
    May JESUS CHRIST be praised.
O hark to what it sings,
As joyously it rings,
    May JESUS CHRIST be praised.

My tongue shall never tire
Of chanting with the choir
    May JESUS CHRIST be praised.
This song of sacred joy,
It never seems to cloy;
    May JESUS CHRIST be praised.

When sleep her balm denies,
My silent spirit sighs
    May JESUS CHRIST be praised.
When evil thoughts molest,
With this I shield my breast,
    May JESUS CHRIST be praised.

Does sadness fill my mind?
A solace here I find,
    May JESUS CHRIST be praised.
Or fades my earthly bliss?
My comfort still is this,
    May JESUS CHRIST be praised.

The night becomes as day,
When from the heart we say
    May JESUS CHRIST be praised.
The powers of darkness fear,
When this sweet chant they hear,
    May JESUS CHRIST be praised.

In Heaven's eternal bliss
The loveliest strain is this,
    May JESUS CHRIST be praised.
Let earth, and sea, and sky
From depth to height reply
    May JESUS CHRIST be praised.

Be this, while life is mine,
My canticle divine,
   May Jesus Christ be praised:
Be this the eternal song,
Through ages all along,
   May Jesus Christ be praised.
                Amen.

8

Now the day is over,
  Night is drawing nigh,
Shadows of the evening
  Steal across the sky.

Now the darkness gathers,
  Stars begin to peep,
Birds, and beasts, and flowers
  Soon will be asleep.

Jesu, give the weary
  Calm and sweet repose,
With thy tenderest blessing
  May our eyelids close.

Grant to little children
  Visions bright of Thee,
Guard the sailors tossing
  On the deep blue sea.

Comfort every sufferer
  Watching late in pain,
Those who plan some evil,
  From their sin restrain.

Through the long night watches
  May Thine Angels spread
Their white wings above me,
  Watching round my bed.

When the morning wakens,
    Then may I arise
Pure, and fresh, and sinless
    In Thy Holy Eyes.

Glory to the FATHER,
    Glory to the SON,
And to Thee, Blest SPIRIT,
    Whilst all ages run.—Amen.

9

O Saving Victim, opening wide
The gate of heaven to Man below,
Our foes press on from every side,
Thine aid supply, Thy strength bestow.

All praise and thanks to Thee ascend,
For evermore, Blest ONE IN THREE;
O grant us life that shall not end
In our true native land with Thee.
                          Amen.

10

All shall call thee Blessed—
Age to age shall tell
GOD the FATHER's message
Sent by Gabriel,—
Graced by GOD the SPIRIT,
GOD the SON's Abode—
All shall call thee Blessed,
Mother of our GOD.

Blessed, for thou barest,
JESUS in thy womb:
Blessed from the manger,
Onward to the tomb,
And since thou returnedst,
To Saint John's abode—
All shall call thee Blessed,
Mother of our GOD.

Thinking how the glory
Of the Highest, sat
Overshadowing Mary,
Our Magnificat
Echoes her's, as meekly
From her voice it flowed:
All shall call thee Blessed,
Mother of our GOD.

Hath not GOD Almighty
Done for thee great things?
Making thee the Mother
Of the King of Kings?
Thou the first to know Him
Veiled in flesh and blood!—
All shall call thee Blessed,
Mother of our GOD.

Yet a higher glory,
Yet a fairer crown,
Shines for ever o'er thee,
Than that sweet renown;
For thou wast obedient
To the Heavenly Word!
All shall call thee Blessed,
Mother of our GOD.

But Thy praise, O JESUS,
Loftier songs employ,
Hearts for Thee exulting,
Leap within for joy,
Joy that GOD the FATHER
Sent Thee from above,
Joy for the o'ershadowing,
Of the SPIRIT's Love.—Amen.

11

A'leluia! sing to JESUS,
  His the sceptre, His the throne:

Alleluia! His the triumph,
  His the victory alone ;
Hark! the songs of peaceful Sion
  Thunder like a mighty flood ;
JESUS out of every nation
  Hath redeemed us by His Blood.

Alleluia! not as orphans
  We are left in sorrow now ;
Alleluia! He is near us,
  Faith believes, nor questions how:
Though the cloud from sight received
     Him,
  When the forty days were o'er,
Shall our hearts forget His promise,
  "I am with you evermore?"

Alleluia! Bread of angels,
  Thou on earth our Food, our Stay,
Alleluia! here the sinful
  Flee to Thee from day to day ;
Intercessor, Friend of sinners,
  Earth's Redeemer, plead for me,
Where the songs of all the sinless
  Sweep across the crystal sea.

Alleluia! King Eternal,
  Thee the Lord of lords we own ;
Alleluia! born of Mary,   [Throne:
  Earth Thy footstool, Heaven Thy
Thou within the veil hast entered,
  Robed in flesh, our great High Priest:
Thou on earth both Priest and Victim
  In the Eucharistic Feast.

Alleluia! sing to JESUS,
  His the sceptre, His the throne ;
Alleluia! His the triumph,
  His the victory alone ;

Hark! the songs of peaceful Sion
  Thunder like a mighty flood;
Jesus out of every nation
  Hath redeemed us by His Blood.
—Amen.

12

Shall we not love thee, Mother dear,
  Whom Jesus loves so well?
And to His glory, year by year,
  Thy joy and honour tell?

Bound with the curse of sin and shame,
  We helpless sinners lay,
Until in tender love He came
  To bear the curse away.

And thee He chose from whom to take
  True flesh His Flesh to be;
In it to suffer for our sake,
  By it to make us free.

Thy Babe He lay upon thy breast,
  To thee He cried for food;
Thy gentle nursing soothed to rest
  Th' Incarnate Son of God.

O wondrous depth of grace Divine
  That He should bend so low:
And Mary, oh, what joy 'twas thine
  In His dear love to know;

Joy to be Mother of the Lord,
  And thine the truer bliss,
In every thought, and deed, and word
  To be for ever His.

And as He loves thee, Mother dear,
  We too will love thee well;

And to His glory, year by year,
  Thy joy and honour tell.

Jesu, the Virgin's Holy Son,
  We praise Thee and adore,
Who art, with God the Father, One
  and Spirit evermore.—Amen.

13

Jerusalem on high
  My song and city is,
My home whene'er I die,
  The centre of my bliss:
    O happy place!
      When shall I be,
      My God, with Thee,
    To see Thy face?

There dwells my Lord my King,
  Judged here unfit to live;
There angels to Him sing,
  And lowly homage give:
    O happy place! &c.

The Patriarchs of old
  There from their travels cease;
The Prophets there behold
  Their longed-for Prince of Peace
    O happy place, &c.

The Lamb's Apostles there
  I might with joy behold,
The harpers I might hear
  Harping on harps of gold;
    O happy place, &c.

The bleeding Martyrs, they
  Within these courts are found,
Clothed in pure array,
  Their scars with glory crowned;
    O happy place, &c.

Ah me! ah me! that I
  In Kedar's tents here stay;
No place like that on high;
  LORD, thither guide my way
    O happy place, &c.
—Amen.

14

Thy kingdom come, O GOD,
  Thy reign, O CHRIST, begin;
Break with Thine iron rod
  The tyrannies of sin.

Where is Thy rule of peace,
  And purity, and love?
When shall all hatred cease,
  As in the realms above?

When comes the promised time
  That war shall be no more,
Oppression, lust, and crime
  Shall flee Thy Face before?

We pray Thee, LORD, arise,
  And come in Thy great might;
Revive our longing eyes,
  Which languish for Thy sight.

Men scorn Thy sacred Name,
  And wolves devour Thy fold;
By many deeds of shame
  We learn that love grows cold.

O'er heathen lands afar
  Thick darkness broodeth yet;
Arise, O Morning Star,
  Arise, and never set.
—Amen.

15

O Mother dear, Jerusalem!
   When shall I come to thee?
When shall my sorrows have an end?
   Thy joys when shall I see?
O happy harbour of GOD's saints!
   O sweet and pleasant soil!
In Thee no sorrow can be found,
   Nor grief, nor care, nor toil.

No murky cloud o'ershadows Thee,
   Nor gloom, nor darksome night;
But every soul shines as the sun;
   For GOD Himself gives light.
O my sweet home, Jerusalem!
   Thy joys when shall I see?
The King that sitteth on thy throne
   In His felicity?

Thy gardens and thy goodly walks
   Continually are green,
Where grow such sweet and pleasant [flowers
   As nowhere else are seen.
Right through thy streets, with pleasing [sound,
   The living waters flow,
And on the banks on either side,
   The trees of life do grow.

Those trees each month yield ripened [fruit;
   For evermore they spring,
And all the nations of the earth
   To thee their honours bring.
O Mother dear, Jerusalem!
   When shall I come to thee?
When shall my sorrows have an end?
   Thy joys when shall I see?—Amen.

16

The day is past and over:
   All thanks, O LORD, to Thee!
I pray Thee that offenceless
   The hours of dark may be.
O JESUS, keep me in Thy sight,
And save me through the coming night

The joys of day are over;
   I lift my heart to Thee;
And call on Thee that sinless
   The hours of gloom may be.
O JESUS, make their darkness light,
And save me through the coming night!

The toils of day are over;
   I raise the hymn to Thee,
And ask that free from peril
   The hours of fear may be.
O JESUS, keep me in Thy sight, [night!
And guard me through the coming

Lighten mine eyes, O SAVIOUR,
   Or sleep in death shall I,
And he, my wakeful tempter,
   Triumphantly shall cry
"Against him I have now prevailed:
Rejoice! the child of GOD has failed."

Be Thou my soul's Preserver,
   O GOD, for Thou dost know
How many are the perils
   Through which I have to go;
O loving JESUS, hear my call,
And guard and save me from them all!
                      Amen.

17

FOR ADVENT.

GOD the FATHER, hear us,
GOD the SAVIOUR, hear us,
HOLY SPIRIT, hear us,
Miserere nobis.

By Thy Incarnation,
By Thy Life and Passion,
Miserere JESU,
Miserere nobis.

Virgin Son of Mary,
Who though GOD wert hiding
In her womb abiding,
Miserere nobis.

In the Holy Manger,
Whilst in Egypt, Stranger
Fleeing there from danger,
Miserere nobis.

By Thy Circumcision,
First drops of remission
For man's lost condition,
Miserere nobis.

By Thy lowly toiling,
Joseph's trade acquiring,
Labor sanctifying,
Miserere nobis.

Come that day of mourning,
Worlds in ashes burning,
JESU to us turning,
Miserere nobis.
—Amen.

18

Hail the Sign, the Sign of JESUS,
 Bright and royal Tree!
Standard of the Monarch, planted
 First on Calvary.

CHORUS:
 Hail the Sign all signs excelling,
  Hail the Sign all ills dispelling,
 Hail the Sign Hell's power quelling,
  Cross of CHRIST, all hail!

Hail the Sign the King preceding,
 Key to Hell's domain!
Lo, the brazen gates it shatters,
 Bars it snaps in twain.—CHO.

Sign to Martyrs strength and refuge,
 Sign to Saints so dear,
Sign by evil men abhorred,
 Sign which devils fear!—CHO.

Sign which on the Day of vengeance,
 Meteor-like shall flare!
Shuddering flesh shall then behold it
 Steeped in bloodred glare.—CHO.

Men shall shriek for very anguish,
 Evil hearts shall quail;
But the Saints in fullest rapture
 Shall that vision hail.—CHO.

Lo, the Cross of CHRIST my Master
 On my brow I trace;
May it keep my mind unsullied,
 Doubt and fear displace.—CHO.

Lo, upon my lips I mark it,
 Sign of JESUS slain;

Christian lips should never utter
    Words impure or vain.—Cho.

Lo, I sign the Sign of JESUS
    Meekly on my breast;
May it guard my heart when living,
    Dying be its rest.—Cho.

In the Name of GOD the FATHER,
    Name of GOD the SON,
Name of GOD the BLESSED SPIRIT,
    Ever Three in ONE.—Cho.—Amen.

19

The hours of day are over,
    The evening calls us home;
Once more to Thee, O FATHER,
    With thankful hearts we come;
For all Thy countless blessings
    We praise Thy holy Name,
And own Thy love unchanging,
    Through days and years the same.

But these, O LORD, can show us
    Thy goodness but in part;
Thy love would lead us onward
    To know Thee as Thou art;
Thy SON came down from Heaven
    To take away our sin,
Thy SPIRIT dwells among us
    To make us clean within.

For this, O LORD, we bless Thee,
    For this we thank Thee most—
The cleansing of the sinful,
    The saving of the lost:
The Teacher ever present,
    The Friend for ever nigh,
The home prepared by JESUS
    For us beyond the sky!

Lord, gather all Thy children
   To meet Thee there at last,
When earthly tasks are ended,
   And earthly days are past:
With all our dear ones round us
   In that eternal home,
Where death no more shall part us,
   And night shall never come!—Amen.

20

O day of rest and gladness,
   O day of joy and light,
O balm of care and sadness,
   Most beautiful, most bright;
On thee the high and lowly,
   Through ages joined in tune,
Sing, Holy, Holy, Holy,
   To the great God Triune.

On thee, at the creation,
   The light had first its birth;
On thee, for our salvation,
   Christ rose from depths of earth;
On thee, our Lord victorious
   The Spirit sent from Heaven;
And thus on thee most glorious
   A triple light was given.

Thou art a port protected
   From storms that round us rise;
A garden intersected
   With streams of paradise;
Thou art a cooling fountain
   In life's dry dreary sand;
From thee, like Pisgah's mountain,
   We view the promised land.

Thou art a holy ladder
   Where Angels go and come;

Each Sunday finds us glad'er,
   Nearer to Heaven, our home:
A day of sweet refection
   Thou art, a day of love;
A day of resurrection
   From earth to things above.

To-day on weary nations
   The heavenly Manna falls;
To holy convocations
   The silver trumpet calls;
Where Gospel-light is glowing
   With pure and radient beams,
And living water flowing
   With soul-refreshing streams.

New graces ever gaining
   From this, our day of rest,
We reach the rest remaining
   To spirits of the blest.
To HOLY GHOST be praises,
   To FATHER and to SON:
The Church her voice upraises
   To Thee, blest THREE in ONE.
                         —Amen.

21

What Child is This, Who laid to rest
   On Mary's lap is sleeping?
Whom angels greet with anthems sweet,
   While shepherds watch are keeping.
This, This is CHRIST the King;
   Whom shepherds guard and angels sing;
Haste, haste to bring Him laud,
   The Babe, the SON of Mary!

Why lies He in such mean estate,
   Where ox and ass are feeding?
Good Christian fear, for sinners here,
   The silent Word is pleading:

Nails, spear, shall pierce Him through,
    The Cross be borne, for me, for you;
Hail, hail the Word made flesh
    The Babe, the Son of Mary.

So bring Him incense, gold and myrrh,
    Come peasant, king, to own Him:
The King of kings, salvation brings,
    Let loving hearts enthrone Him.
Raise, raise the song on high,
    The Virgin sings her lullaby:
Joy, joy, for Christ is born,
    The Babe, the Son of Mary!—Amen.

22

Hail to the Lord's Anointed,
    Great David's greater Son;
Hail, in the time appointed,
    His reign on earth begun!
He comes to break oppression,
    To set the captive free;
To take away transgression,
    And rule in equity.

He shall come down like showers
    Upon the fruitful earth,
And joy and hope, like flowers,
    Spring in His path to birth;
Before Him on the mountains
    Shall Peace, the herald, go;
From hill to vale the fountains
    Of righteousness o'erflow.

Kings shall bow down before Him,
    And gold and incense bring;
All nations shall adore Him,
    His praise all people sing;
To Him shall prayer unceasing,
    And daily vows ascend;

His kingdom still increasing,
　A kingdom without end.

O'er every foe victorious,
　He on His throne shall rest;
From age to age more glorious,
　All-blessing and all-blessed;
The tide of time shall never
　His covenant remove;
His name shall stand for ever,
　His changeless Name of love.
　　　　　　　　—Amen.

23

In the wintry heaven,
　Shines a wondrous star;
In the East the wise men
　Watched it from afar;
Asking, "Why this lustre
　So unearthly bright?"
Answering, "CHRIST in glory
　Comes to earth to-night."

O'er the dusty highway
　O'er the deserts drear,
From the East the wise men,
　Watched it shining clear;
Asking, "Shall we follow
　In this starlight way?"
Answering, "Yes, 'twill lead us
　To the perfect day."

In a lonely manger
　Lies an Infant weak;
Is it He whom wise men
　Came so far to seek?
Asking, "Where the Monarch?
　Where Judea's King?"
Saying, "Gifts and worship
　To His throne we bring."

In our hearts, we children,
   See this star once more :
Not as wise men saw it,
   In the days of yore.
Asking, " May we bring Him
   Childhood's love to-day ? "
Answering, " Come, dear children
   JESUS says we may."—Amen.

24

The snow lay on the ground,
   The stars shone bright.
When CHRIST our LORD was born
   On Christmas night.
Venite adoremus
   Dominum ;
Venite adoremus
   Dominum.
CHO.—Venite, &c.

'Twas Mary, daughter pure
   Of holy Ann,
That brought into this world
   The GOD-made-MAN ;
She laid Him in a Stall
   At Bethlehem,
The ass and oxen shared
   The roof with them.
CHO.—Venite, &c.

Saint Joseph, too, was by
   To tend the Child :
To guard Him and protect
   His Mother mild :
The angels hovered round
   And sang this song,
Venite adoremus
   Dominum.
—CHO.—Venite, &c.

And then that manger poor
  Became a Throne,
For He Whom Mary bore,
  Was GOD the SON.
O come then let us join
  The heavenly host,
And praise the FATHER, SON,
  And HOLY GHOST.
CHO.—Venite, &c.—Amen.

25

Do no sinful action,
  Speak no sinful word;
Ye belong to JESUS,
  Children of the LORD.

CHRIST is kind and gentle,
  CHRIST is pure and true,
And His little children
  Must be holy too.

There's a wicked spirit
  Watching round you still,
And he tries to tempt you
  To all harm and ill.

But ye must not hear him,
  Though 'tis hard for you
To resist the evil,
  And the good to do.

For ye promised truly,
  In your infant days,
To renounce him wholly,
  And forsake his ways.

Ye are new-born Christians;
  Ye must learn to fight
With the bad within you,
  And to do the right.

CHRIST is your own Master
　　He is good and true,
And His little children
　　Must be holy too.—Amen.

26

Stand up, stand up for JESUS,
　　Ye soldiers of the Cross;
Lift high the Royal Banner,
　　It must not suffer loss;
From victory unto victory
　　His army shall be led,
'Till every foe is vanquished
　　And CHRIST is LORD indeed.

Stand up, stand up for JESUS,
　　Stand in His strength alone;
The arm of flesh will fail you,
　　Ye dare not trust your own.
Put on the Gospel armor,
　　And, watching unto prayer,
When duty calls, or danger,
　　Be never wanting there.

Stand up, stand up for JESUS,
　　The strife will not be long;
This day the noise of battle,
　　The next, the victor's song,
To him that overcometh
　　A crown of life shall be;
He with the King of glory
　　Shall reign eternally.

27

JESU, my LORD, my GOD, my all!
How can I love Thee as I ought?
And how revere this wondrous Gift,
So far surpassing hope or thought?

Sweet Sacrament, we Thee adore!
O make us love Thee more and more.

Had I but Mary's stainless heart
To love Thee with, my dearest King,
O with what bursts of fervent praise
Thy goodness, JESU, would I sing.
 Sweet Sacrament, &c.

O see within a creature's hand
The vast CREATOR deigns to be,
Reposing, infant-like, as though
On Joseph's arm or Mary's knee.
 Sweet Sacrament, &c.

The Body, Soul, and GODHEAD all!
O Mystery of Love divine!
I cannot compass all I have,
For all Thou hast and art are mine!
 Sweet Sacrament, &c. —Amen.

28

Nearer, my GOD, to Thee,
 Nearer to Thee;
E'en though it be a cross
 That raiseth me,
Still all my song shall be,
Nearer, my GOD, to Thee,
 Nearer to Thee!

Though, like a wanderer,
 The sun gone down,
Darkness comes over me,
 My rest a stone:
Yet in my dreams I'd be
Nearer, my GOD, to Thee,
 Nearer to Thee!

There let my way appear
 Steps unto heaven:
All that Thou sendest me
 In mercy given;

Angels to beckon me
Nearer, my GOD, to Thee,
Nearer to Thee!

Then, with my waking thoughts,
Bright with Thy praise,
Out of my stony griefs
Bethel I'll raise;
So, by my woes to be
Nearer, my GOD, to Thee,
Nearer to Thee!—Amen.

29

O JESU! it was surely sweet
To sit and listen at Thy Feet,
With those who in Thy life drew near
Thy words of love and grace to hear.

And sweet it was to walk with Thee
Beside the lake of Galilee;
Or, safe embarked in Peter's boat,
O'er its blue waves with Thee to float.

But sweeter far it is to pray
Before Thine Altar-throne to-day,
And feel the love that bids Thee lie
Thus wrapped in holiest mystery.

Hail! JESU! hail! my dearest LORD,
By Seraph choirs in Heaven adored;
Hail! JESU! Who art hidden thus
On this poor earth for love of us.—Amen.

30

I am a faithful Catholic,
I love my blessed faith;
I will be true to Holy Church,
And steadfast unto death.

The lawful pastors of the Church
Right gladly I obey;

Nor heed the guileful words of those
  Who fain would make me stray.

I love the Altar where I kneel
  My JESUS to adore;
I love His Mother and His Saints—
  Oh, may I love them more!

I love the Cross, I love my books,
  Each thing that tells of faith:
Let foolish men rail as they will,
  I'll love them unto death.—Amen.

31

We love the place, O GOD,
  Wherein Thine honour dwells;
The joy of Thine abode
  All earthly joy excels.

It is the house of prayer,
  Wherein Thy servants meet;
And Thou, O LORD, art there
  Thy chosen flock to greet.

We love the sacred Font;
  For there the Holy DOVE
To pour is ever wont
  His blessing from above.

We love Thine Altar, LORD;
  Oh, what on earth so dear?
For there, in faith adored,
  We find Thy Presence near.

We love the Word of life,
  The Word that tells of peace,
Of comfort in the strife,
  And joys that never cease.

We love to sing below
   For mercies freely given;
But oh! we long to know
   The triumph-song of heaven.

LORD JESUS, give us grace
   On earth to love Thee more,
In heaven to see Thy Face,
   And with Thy Saints adore.
               —Amen

32

SAVIOUR, like a Shepherd lead us,
   Much we need Thy tender care;
In Thy pleasant pastures feed us,
   For our use Thy fold prepare.
Blessed JESUS! Blessed JESUS!
   Thou hast bought us, Thine we are.

We are Thine, do Thou befriend us,
   Be the Guardian of our way;
Keep Thy flock; from sin defend us,
   Seek us when we go astray,
Blessed JESUS! Blessed JESUS!
   Hear Thy children when they pray.

At the Font Thou didst receive us,
   Made Thy children then by Thee;
Thou had'st mercy to relieve us,
   Grace to cleanse, and power to free.
Blessed JESUS! Blessed JESUS!
   Early were we brought to Thee.

Early let us seek Thy favour,
   Early let us do Thy will,
Blessed LORD and only SAVIOUR,
   With Thyself our bosoms fill.
Blessed JESUS! Blessed JESUS!
   Thou hast loved us—love us still.
               —Amen.

33

The sun is sinking fast,
    The daylight dies ;
Let love awake, and pay
    Her evening sacrifice.

As CHRIST upon the Cross
    His head inclined,
And to His FATHER's hands
    His parting soul resign'd ;

So now herself my soul
    Would wholly give
Into His sacred charge,
    In Whom all spirits live ;

So now beneath His eye
    Would calmly rest,
Without a wish or thought
    Abiding in the breast ;

Save that His will be done,
    Whate'er betide ;
Dead to herself, and dead
    In Him to all beside.

Thus would I live : yet now
    Not I, but He,
In all His power and love,
    Henceforth alive in me.

One Sacred Trinity,
    One LORD Divine,
May I be ever His,
    And He for ever mine.—Amen.

34

Rejoice, rejoice, believers!
    And let your lights appear ;
The evening is advancing,
    And darker night is near.

The Bridegroom is arising,
  And soon He will draw nigh;
Up! pray, and watch, and wrestle!
  At midnight comes the cry.

See that your lamps are burning,
  Replenish them with oil;
Look now for your salvation,
  The end of sin and toil.
The watchers on the mountain
  Proclaim the Bridegroom near,
Go meet Him as He cometh,
  With alleluias clear.

O wise and holy virgins,
  Now raise your voices higher,
Till in your jubilations,
  Ye meet the angel choir.
The marriage feast is waiting,
  The gates wide open stand;
Up, up, ye heirs of glory!
  The Bridegroom is at hand.

Our hope and expectation,
  O JESUS, now appear;
Arise, Thou Sun so longed for,
  O'er this benighted sphere!
With hearts and hands uplifted,
  We plead, O LORD, to see
The day of earth's redemption,
  And ever be with Thee!
              —Amen.

35

Lead, kindly Light, amid the encircling
        Lead Thou me on; [gloom,
The night is dark, and I am far from
        Lead Thou me on. [home,

Keep Thou my feet ; I do not ask to see
The distant scene ; one step enough for
    me.

I was not ever thus, nor prayed that Thou
        Shouldst lead me on ;
I loved to choose and see my path ; but
        now
    Lead Thou me on.
I loved the garish day, and, spite of
        fears,
Pride ruled my will : remember not past
        years.

So long Thy power hath blest me, sure it
        still
        Will lead me on
O'er moor and fen, o'er crag and torrent,
        till
        The night is gone,
And with the morn those angel faces
        smile,
Which I have loved long since, and lost
        awhile.
                        —Amen.

36

Daily, daily sing the praises
  Of the city GOD hath made ;
In the beauteous fields of Eden
  Its foundation-stones are laid.

CHORUS.

O that I had wings of angels,
  Here to spread and heavenward fly;
I would seek the gates of Zion,
  Far beyond the starry sky!

All the walls of that dear City
   Are of bright and burnished gold;
It is matchless in its beauty,
   And its treasures are untold.—Cho.

In the midst of that dear City
   Christ is reigning on His seat;
And the angels swing their censers
   In a ring about His Feet.—Cho.

From thé Throne a river issues,
   Clear as crystal, passing bright,
And it traverses the City
   Like a sudden beam of light.—Cho.

There the meadows green and dewy
   Shine with lilies wondrous fair;
Thousands, thousands are the colours
   Of the waving flowers there. Cho.

There the wind is sweetly fragrant,
   And is laden with the song
Of the Seraphs. and the Elders,
   And the great Redeemed Throng.Cho.

O I would my ears were open
   Here to catch that happy strain!
O I would my eyes some vision
   Of that Eden could attain. Cho.
                —Amen.

37

Forth to the fight, ye ransomed,
   Mighty in God's own might,
Storming the tide of battle,
   Routing the hosts of night.

       Chorus.

Lift ye the Blood-red banner,
   Wield ye the victor's sword
Raise ye the Christian's war cry—
   "The Cross of Christ the Lord."

Fear not the din of battle,
  Follow where He has trod,
Perfecting strength in weakness-
  JESUS, incarnate GOD.—CHO.

Angels around us hover,
  Succour in time of need,
Ever at hand to strengthen,
  Guardians they, indeed.—CHO.

Arm ye against the battle,
  Watch ye, and fast and pray,
Peace shall succeed the warfare,
  Night shall be changed to day.—CHO.

Fight, for the LORD is o'er you.
  Fight, for He bids you fight,
There, where the fray is thickest,
  Close with the hosts of night.—CHO.
                              —Amen.

38

"Come unto Me, ye weary,
  And I will give you rest."
O blessed voice of JESUS,
  Which comes to hearts opprest!
It tells of benediction,
  Or pardon, grace and peace;
Of joy that hath no ending,
  Of love which cannot cease.

"Come unto me, dear children,
  And I will give you light."
O loving voice of JESUS,
  Which comes to cheer the night!
Our hearts were filled with sadness,
  And we had lost our way,
But morning brings us gladness,
  And songs the break of day.

(35)

"Come unto Me, ye fainting,
  And I will give you life."
O peaceful voice of JESUS,
  Which comes to end our strife!
The foe is stern and eager,
  The fight is fierce and long;
But Thou hast made us mighty,
  And stronger than the strong.

"And whosover cometh,
  I will not cast him out."
O patient voice of JESUS,
  Which drives away our doubt!
Which calls us, very sinners,
  Unworthy though we be
Of love so free and boundless,
  To come, dear LORD, to Thee.
        —Amen.

39

I'm but a stranger here,
  Heav'n is my home;
Earth is a desert drear,
  Heav'n is my home.
Danger and sorrow stand
  Round me on ev'ry hand;
Heav'n is my fatherland,
  Heav'n is my home.

What tho' the tempest rage,
  Heav'n is my home;
Short is my pilgrimage,
  Heav'n is my home.
And Time's wild wintry blast
  Soon will be over-past;
I shall reach home at last,
  Heav'n is my home.

Therefore I murmur not;
  Heav'n is my home;
Whate'er my earthly lot,
  Heav'n is my home.
And I shall surely stand
  There at my LORD's right hand;
Heav'n is my father-land,
  Heav'n is my home.
                              —Amen.

40

I heard the voice of JESUS say,
  "Come unto me and rest;
Lay down, thou weary one, lay down
  Thy head upon my breast!"
I came to JESUS as I was,
  Weary, and worn, and sad;
I found in Him a resting-place,
  And He has made me glad.

I heard the voice of JESUS say,
  "Behold I freely give
The living water; thirsty one,
  Stoop down, and drink, and live:"
I came to JESUS, and I drank
  Of that life-giving stream;
My thirst was quenched, my soul revived,
  And now I live in Him.

I heard the voice of JESUS say,
  "I am this dark world's Light:
Look unto me, thy morn shall rise,
  And all thy day be bright:"
I looked to JESUS, and I found
  In Him my Star, my Sun;
And in that Light of life I'll walk
  Till travelling days are done.
                              Amen.

41

When I survey the wondrous Cross
   On which the Prince of Glory died,
My richest gain I count but loss,
   And pour contempt on all my pride.

Forbid it, LORD, that I should boast,
   Save in the Cross of Christ, my GOD:
All the vain things that charm me most,
   I sacrifice them to Thy blood.

See, from His head, His hands, His feet,
   Sorrow and love flow mingled down!
Did e'er such love and sorrow meet?
   Or thorns compose a SAVIOUR's crown?

Were the whole realm of nature mine,
   That were a tribute far too small;
Love so amazing, so divine,
   Demands my life, my soul, my all.
                    —Amen.

42

My faith looks up to Thee,
Thou Lamb of Calvary,
   SAVIOUR divine!
Now hear me while I pray;
Take all my guilt away;
O let me from this day
   Be wholly Thine.

May Thy rich grace impart
Strength to my fainting heart,
   My zeal inspire;
As Thou hast died for me,
O may my love to Thee
Pure, warm, and changeless be,
   A living fire.

While life's dark maze I tread,
And griefs around me spread,
  Be Thou my Guide:
Bid darkness turn to day;
Wipe sorrow's tears away,
Nor let me ever stray
  From Thee aside.

When ends life's transient dream,
When death's cold, sullen stream
  Shall o'er me roll,
Blest SAVIOUR, then in love,
Fear and distrust remove;
O bear me safe above,
  A ransom'd soul.—Amen.

43

JESUS calls us; o'er the tumult
  Of our life's wild, restless sea,
Day by day His sweet voice soundeth,
  Softly, clearly, Follow Me.

JESUS calls us, from the evil
  In a world we cannot flee,
From each idol that would keep us,
  Softly, clearly, Follow Me.

Still in joy, and still in sadness,
  We discern His own decree:
Still He calls, in cares and pleasures,
  Softly, clearly, Follow Me.

As Saint Andrew heard Thee, SAVIOUR,
  By the lake of Galilee,
May we hear, and help each other
  Day by day to follow Thee.

Thou dost call us! May we ever
  To Thy call attentive be:
Give our hearts to Thine obedience,
  Leave all, rise, and follow Thee!
                    Amen.

44

To CHRIST, the Prince of peace,
   And SON of GOD most high,
The FATHER of the world to come,
   We lift our joyful cry.

Deep in His Heart for us
   The wound of love He bore,
That love which He enkindles still
   In hearts that Him adore.

O JESU, Victim Blest,
   What else but love Divine
Could Thee constrain to open thus
   That Sacred Heart of Thine?

O wondrous Fount of love,
   O Well of waters free,
O heavenly Flame, refining Fire,
   O burning Charity!

Hide us in Thy dear Heart,
   JESU, our SAVIOUR Blest,
So shall we find Thy plenteous grace,
   And heaven's eternal rest.—Amen.

45

Thee we adore, O hidden SAVIOUR, Thee,
Who in Thy Sacrament dost deign to be;
Both flesh and spirit at Thy Presence fail,
Yet here Thy Presence we devoutly hail.

O blest Memorial of our dying LORD,
Who living Bread to men doth here afford!

O may our souls forever feed on Thee,
  And Thou, O CHRIST, forever precious be.
Fountain of goodness, JESU, LORD and GOD,
Cleanse us, unclean, with Thy most cleansing Blood;
Increase our faith and love, that we may know
The hope and peace which from Thy Presence flow.

O CHRIST, Whom now beneath a veil we see,
May what we thirst for soon our portion be,
To gaze on Thee unveiled, and see Thy Face,
The vision of Thy glory and Thy grace.
—Amen.

46

Spouse of CHRIST, in arms contending
  O'er each clime beneath the sun,
Blend with prayers for help ascending,
  Notes of praise for triumph won.

CHORUS.

Holy Mother of the Faithful,
  Thy faith shall never fail,
And the gates of hell against Thee,
  Never, never shall prevail.

Mary leads the sacred story,
  Mary with her heavenly Child,
Sharer with Him now in glory,
  Maid and mother undefiled.—CHO.

Angels next, in due gradation
  Of the ninefold ministry,
Hymn the FATHER of Creation,
  Maker of the stars on high.—Cho.

John, the herald voice sonorous,
  More than prophet own'd to be,
Patriarchs and seers in chorus
  Swell the angelic harmony.—Cho.

Near to CHRIST, the Apostles seated,
  Trampling on the powers of hell,
By the promise now completed,
  Judge the tribes of Israel.—Cho.

They who nobly died believing,
  Martyrs purpled in their gore,
Crowns of life by death receiving,
  Rest in joy for evermore.—Cho.

Priests and Deacons, Gospel preachers,
  And Confessors numberless,
Prelates meek, and holy teachers,
  Bear the palm of righteousness.—Cho.

Lo, in bridal pomp, fair virgins,
  To the Lamb, all consecrate,
Haste with lilies and with roses,
  On the Bridegroom's steps to wait.
               —Cho.

All are blest together, praising
  God's eternal majesty;
Thrice repeated anthems raising
  To the all-holy Trinity.—Cho.

So may we, with hearts devoted,
  Serve our God in holiness;
So may we, by God promoted,
  Share that Heaven which they possess.
               —Cho.—Amen

47

FOR LENT.

God the FATHER, hear us,
God the SAVIOUR, hear us,
HOLY SPIRIT, hear us,
Miserere nobis.

By the Baptist's preaching,
And Thy Holy teaching,
John's Baptism seeking,
Miserere nobis.

By Thy tribulation,
Fasting, and temptation,
Conquest over Satan,
Miserere nobis.

By Thy Mercy's dealing,
With the sinner kneeling,
By Thy words of healing,
Miserere nobis.

By Thy bitter crying,
In the garden lying,
By Thy love undying,
Miserere nobis.

By the Chalice filling,
Blood of Thine own spilling,
Paschal Victim willing,
Miserere nobis.

Hear us guilty moaning,
Our offenses owning,
By Thy love atoning,
Miserere nobis.
—Amen.

48

What a Friend we have in JESUS,
　All our sins and griefs to bear!
What a privilege to carry
　Everything to GOD in prayer!
Oh, what peace we often forfeit,
　Oh, what needless pain we bear—
All because we do not carry
　Everything to GOD in prayer!

Have we trials and temptations?
　Is there trouble anywhere?
We should never be discouraged;
　Take it to the LORD in prayer.
Can we find a friend so faithful,
　Who will all our sorrows share?
JESUS knows our every weakness—
　Take it to the LORD in prayer.

Are we weak and heavy-laden,
　Cumbered with a load of care?
Rest on Him thy spirit's burden—
　Take it to the LORD in prayer;
Do thy friends despise, forsake thee?
　Take it to the LORD in prayer:
In His arms He'll take and shield thee,
　Thou wilt find thy solace there.
　　　　　　　　　　　—Amen.

49

Beneath the Cross of JESUS
　I fain would take my stand
The shadow of a mighty rock,
　Within a weary land.
A home within the wilderness,
　A rest upon the way,
From the burning of the noontide heat,
　And the burden of the day.

O safe and happy shelter,
  O refuge tried and sweet,
O trysting-place where heaven's love
  And heaven's justice meet.
As to the holy Patriarch
  That wondrous dream was given,
So seems my SAVIOUR's Cross to me—
  A ladder up to heaven.

There lies beneath its shadow,
  But on the further side,
The darkness of an awful grave
  That gapes both deep and wide;
And there between us stands the Cross,
  Two arms outstretched to save,
Like a watchman set to guard the way
  From that eternal grave.

Upon that Cross of JESUS
  Mine eye at times can see
The very dying form of One
  Who suffered there for me;
And from my smitten heart with tears,
  Two wonders I confess—
The wonders of His glorious love,
  And my own worthlessness.

I take, O Cross, thy shadow,
  For my abiding place;
I ask no other sunshine
  Than the sunshine of His face;
Content to let the world go by,
  To know no gain nor loss,—
My sinful self my only shame,
  My glory—all the Cross.—Amen.

50

In the hour of trial,
  JESUS, plead for me;
Lest by base denial
  I depart from Thee;

When Thou see'st me waver,
  With a look recall,
Nor for fear or favour
  Suffer me to fall.
With forbidden pleasures
  Would this vain world charm;
Or its sordid treasures
  Spread to work me harm;
Bring to my remembrance
  Sad Gethsemane,
Or, in darker semblance,
  Cross-crown'd Calvary.

Should Thy mercy send me
  Sorrow, toil, and woe:
Or should pain attend me
  On my path below;
Grant that I may never
  Fail Thy hand to see;
Grant that I may ever
  Cast my care on Thee.

When my last hour cometh,
  Fraught with strife and pain,
When my dust returneth
  To the dust again;
On Thy truth relying,
  Through that mortal strife,
Jesus, take me, dying,
  To eternal life.—Amen.

51

Take my life, and let it be
  Consecrated, LORD, to Thee,
Take my moments and my days;
  Let them flow in ceaseless praise.
Take my hands, and let them move
  At the impulse of Thy love.
Take my feet, and let them be
  Swift and "beautiful" for Thee.

Take my voice, and let me sing
   Always, only, for my King.
Take my lips, and let them be
   Filled with messages from Thee.
Take my silver and my gold;
   Not a mite would I withhold.
Take my intellect, and use
   Every power as Thou shalt choose.

Take my will and make it Thine,
   It shall be no longer mine.
Take my heart, it is Thine own;
   It shall be Thy royal throne.
Take my love; my LORD, I pour
   At Thy feet its treasure-store.
Take myself, and I will be
   Ever, only, all for Thee.—Amen.

52

JESUS, I my cross have taken,
   All to leave and follow Thee;
Destitute, despised, forsaken,
   Thou from hence my all shalt be.
Perish every fond ambition,
   All I've sought and hoped, and known,
Yet how rich is my condition,
   God and heaven are still my own.

Let the world despise and leave me
   They have left my SAVIOUR too—
Human hearts and looks deceive me;
   Thou art not, like man, untrue;
And while Thou shalt smile upon me,
   God of wisdom, love, and might,
Foes may hate and friends may shun me;
   Show Thy face, and all is bright.

Go, then, earthly fame and treasures!
   Come disaster, scorn and pain!
In Thy service, pain is pleasure;
   With Thy favour loss is gain.

I have called Thee Abba, Father;
   I have stayed my heart on Thee;
Storms may howl and clouds may gather;
   All must work for good to me.

Take, my soul, thy full salvation;
   Rise o'er sin, and fear, and care;
Joy to find in every station
   Something still to do or bear!
Think what Spirit dwells within thee,—
   What a Father's smile is thine;
What thy SAVIOUR did to win thee,—
   Child of Heaven, should'st thou repine?

Haste thee on from grace to glory
   Armed by faith, and winged by prayer;
Heaven's eternal days before thee;
   GOD's own hand shall guide thee there.
Soon shall close thy earthly mission.
   Swift shall pass thy pilgrim days;
Hope soon change to glad fruition,
   Faith to sight, and prayer to praise.
                      Amen.

53

O JESUS, I have promised
   To serve Thee to the end;
Be Thou for ever near me,
   My Master and my Friend!
I shall not fear the battle
   If Thou art by my side,
Nor wander from the pathway,
   If Thou wilt be my guide.

O let me feel Thee near me—
   The world is ever near:
I see the sights that dazzle,
   The tempting sounds I hear.

My foes are ever near me,
   Around me and within;
But, JESUS, draw Thou nearer,
   And shield my soul from sin.
O let me hear Thee speaking
   In accents clear and still,
Above the storms of passion,
   The murmurs of self-will:
O speak to re-assure me,
   To hasten or control;
O speak, and make me listen,
   Thou Guardian of my soul!
O let me see Thy features,
   The look that once could make
So many a true disciple
   Leave all things for Thy sake;
The look that beamed on Peter
   When he Thy Name denied;
The look that draws Thy lovers
   Close to Thy pierced Side.
O let me see Thy foot-marks,
   And in them plant my own;
My hope to follow duty,
   Is in Thy strength alone.
O guide me, call me, draw me,
   Uphold me to the end;
And then in heaven receive me,
   My SAVIOUR, and my Friend. Amen.

54

O! come to the merciful SAVIOUR who calls you,
   O! come to the LORD who forgives and forgets;
Though dark be the fortune on earth that befalls you,
   A Home waits above, where the sun never sets.

O! come then to JESUS, whose Arms are extended
  To fold His dear children in closest embrace:
O! come, for your exile will shortly be ended,
  And JESUS will show you His beautiful Face.

Yes, come to the SAVIOUR, whose mercy grows brighter
  The longer you look at the depth of His love;
And fear not! 'tis JESUS! and life's cares grow lighter
  In thought of the Home and the Glory above.

O! come then to JESUS, and say how you love Him,
  And vow at His Feet you will keep in His Grace;
For tears that are shed by a sinner can move Him,
  And sins will drop off in His tender embrace.

Come, come to His Feet and lay open your story
  Of suffering and sorrow, of guilt and of shame;
The pardon of sin is the crown of His Glory,
  The joy of our LORD to be true to His Name.
    —Amen.

55

Jesus, the very thought of Thee
  With sweetness fills the breast;
But sweeter far Thy Face to see,
  And in Thy Presence rest.

No voice can sing, no heart can frame,
  Nor can the memory find,
A sweeter sound than Jesus' Name,
  The Saviour of mankind.

O Hope of every contrite heart,
  O Joy of all the meek,
To those who fall, how kind Thou art!
  How good to those who seek!

But what to those who find? Ah! this
  Nor tongue nor pen can show;
The love of Jesus, what it is
  None but His loved ones know.

Jesus, our only Joy be Thou,
  As Thou our Prize wilt be;
In Thee be all our glory now,
  And through eternity.—Amen.

56

Art thou weary, art thou languid,
  Art thou sore distress'd?
"Come to me," saith One, "and coming,
  Be at rest."

Hath He marks to lead me to Him,
  If He be my Guide?
"In His Feet and Hands are wound-
  And His Side."   (prints,

Is there diadem, as Monarch,
  That His Brow adorns?
"Yea, a crown, in very surety,
  But of thorns."

If I find Him, if I follow,
  What His guerdon here?
" Many a sorrow, many a labour,
  Many a tear."

If I still hold closely to Him,
  What hath He at last?
" Sorrow vanquish'd, labour ended,
  Jordan pass'd."

If I ask Him to receive me,
  Will He say me nay?
" Not till earth, and not till heaven
  Pass away."

Finding, following, keeping, struggling,
  Is He sure to bless?
" Saints, Apostles, Prophets, Martyrs,
  Answer, Yes."—Amen.

57

Days and moments quickly flying
  Blend the living with the dead;
Soon will you and I be lying
  Each within our narrow bed.

Soon our souls to GOD Who gave them
  Will have sped their rapid flight;
Able now by grace to save them,
  O, that while we can we might!

JESU, Infinite REDEEMER,
  Maker of this mighty frame,
Teach, O teach us to remember
  What we are, and whence we came;

Whence we came and whither wending
  Soon we must through darkness go,
To inherit bliss unending,
  Or eternity of woe.

As the tree falls, so must it lie;
As the man lives, so will he die;
As the man dies, such must he be,
All through the days of Eternity.
—Amen.

58

My God, my Father, while I stray
Far from my home in life's rough way,
O teach me from my heart to say,
"Thy will be done."

Though dark my path, and sad my lot,
Let me be still and murmur not,
Or breathe the prayer divinely taught,
"Thy will be done."

What though in lonely grief I sigh
For friends beloved no longer nigh,
Submissive would I still reply,
"Thy will be done."

If Thou shouldst call me to resign
What most I prize, it ne'er was mine;
I only yield Thee what is Thine;
"Thy will be done."

Let but my fainting heart be blest
With Thy sweet Spirit for its guest,
My God, to Thee I leave the rest;
"Thy will be done."

Renew my will from day to day,
Blend it with Thine, and take away
All that now makes it hard to say,
"Thy will be done."
—Amen.

59

Work, for the night is coming,
Work, thro' the morning hours;
Work, while the dew is sparkling,
Work, 'mid springing flowers;
Work, when the day grows brighter,
Work, in the glowing sun;
Work, for the night is coming,
When man's work is done.

Work, for the night is coming,
Work, thro' the sunny noon;
Fill brightest hours with labour,
Rest comes sure and soon;
Give every flying minute
Something to keep in store;
Work, for the night is coming,
When man works no more.

Work, for the night is coming,
Under the sunset skies:
While their bright tints are glowing,
Work, for daylight flies:
Work, till the last beam fadeth,
Fadeth to shine no more;
Work, while the night is darkening,
When man's work is o'er.
—Amen.

60

Nearer, my God, to Thee,
  Nearer to Thee,
E'en though it be a cross
  That raiseth me;
Still all my song shall be,
Nearer, my God, to Thee,
  Nearer to Thee!

Deep in Thy Sacred Heart,
   Let me abide,
Thou that hast bled for me.
   Sorrowed and died;
Sweet shall my weeping be,
   Grief surely leading me
Nearer, my GOD, to Thee,
   Nearer to Thee.

Friends may depart from me,
   Night may come down,
Clouds of adversity
   Darken and frown;
Still through my tears I'll see
   Hope gently leading me,
Nearer, my GOD, to Thee,
   Nearer to Thee.—Amen.

61

Once in royal David's City
   Stood a lowly cattle shed,
Where a mother laid her Baby,
   In a manger for His bed:
Mary was that mother mild,
JESUS CHRIST her little Child.

He came down to earth from heaven,
   Who is GOD and LORD of all,
And His shelter was a stable,
   And His cradle was a stall;
With the poor, and mean, and lowly,
Lived on earth our SAVIOUR Holy.

And, through all His wondrous childhood,
   He would honour and obey,
Love, and watch the lowly Maiden,
   In whose gentle arms He lay;
Christian children all must be
Mild, obedient, good as He.

For He is our childhood's Pattern,
  Day by day like us He grew;
He was little, weak, and helpless,
  Tears and smiles like us He knew;
And He feeleth for our sadness,
And He shareth in our gladness.

And our eyes at last shall see Him,
  Through His own redeeming love,
For that Child so dear and gentle
  Is our LORD in heaven above;
And He leads His children on
To the place where He is gone.

Not in that poor lowly stable,
  With the oxen standing by,
We shall see Him: but in heaven,
  Set at GOD's right hand on high;
When like stars His children crowned
All in white shall wait around.—Amen.

62

There is a fountain, filled with Blood
  Drawn from IMMANUEL's veins;
And sinners, plunged beneath that flood,
  Lose all their guilty stains.

The dying thief rejoiced to see
  That fountain in his day;
And there may I, though vile as he,
  Wash all my sins away.

Dear dying Lamb, Thy precious Blood
  Shall never lose its power,
Till all the ransomed Church of GOD
  Be saved to sin no more.

E'er since by faith I saw the stream
  Thy flowing wounds supply,
Redeeming love has been my theme,
  And shall be till I die.

Then in a nobler, sweeter song,
  I'll sing Thy power to save:
When this poor lisping, stammering
      tongue
  Lies silent in the grave.—Amen.

63

For ever with the LORD!
  Amen, so let it be!
Life from the dead is in that word;
  'Tis immortality.

Here in the body pent,
  Absent from Him I roam,
Yet nightly pitch my moving tent
  A day's march nearer home.

My FATHER's house on high,
  Home of my soul, how near
At times to faith's far-seeing eye
  Thy golden gates appear!

Ah, then my spirit faints
  To reach the land I love,
The bright inheritance of saints,
  Jerusalem above.

Yet clouds will intervene,
  And all my prospect flies;
Like Noah's dove, I flit between
  Rough seas and stormy skies.

Anon the clouds depart,
  The winds and waters cease,
And sweetly o'er my gladdened heart
  Expands the bow of peace.

I hear at morn and even,
  At noon and midnight hour,
The choral harmonies of heaven:
  Earth's Babel-tongues o'erpower.

That resurrection word,
  That shout of victory:
Once more, For ever with the LORD;
  Amen, so let it be.—Amen.

64

"Christian! seek not yet repose,"
Hear thy guardian angel say,
Thou art in the midst of foes,
      "Watch and pray."

Principalities and powers,
Mustering their unseen array,
Wait for thy unguarded hours;
      "Watch and pray."

Gird thy heavenly armour on,
Wear it ever night and day;
Ambushed lies the evil one;
      "Watch and pray."

Hear the victors who o'ercame;
Still they mark each warrior's way;
All with one sweet voice exclaim,
      "Watch and pray."

Hear, above all, hear thy LORD,
Him thou lovest to obey;
Hide within thy heart His word,
      "Watch and pray."

Watch, as if on that alone
Hung the issue of the day;
Pray, that help may be sent down;
      "Watch and pray."—Amen.

65

Rock of ages, cleft for me,
Let me hide myself in Thee;
Let the Water and the Blood,
From Thy riven Side which flowed,

Be of sin the double cure,
Cleanse me from its guilt and power.

Not the labours of my hands
Can fulfil Thy law's demands;
Could my zeal no respite know,
Could my tears for ever flow,
All for sin could not atone:
Thou must save, and Thou alone.

Nothing in my hand I bring,
Simply to Thy Cross I cling:
Naked, come to Thee for dress;
Helpless, look to Thee for grace;
Foul, I to the Fountain fly:
Wash me, SAVIOUR, or I die.

While I draw this fleeting breath,
When my eyelids close in death,
When I soar through tracts unknown,
See Thee on Thy Judgment Throne;
Rock of ages, cleft for me,
Let me hide myself in Thee.—Amen.

66

Come, HOLY GHOST, our souls inspire,
And lighten with Celestial Fire;
Thou the Anointing SPIRIT art,
Who dost Thy Sevenfold Gifts impart:
Thy blessed Unction from above
Is Comfort, Life, and Fire of Love;
Enable with Perpetual Light
The dullness of our blinded sight;
Anoint and cheer our soiled face
With the abundance of Thy Grace;
Keep far our foes, give peace at home;
Where Thou art Guide, no ill can come
Teach us to know the FATHER, SON,
And THEE, of Both, to be but ONE;

That, through the ages all along,
This may be our endless song:
> Praise to Thy Eternal Merit,
> FATHER, SON, and HOLY SPIRIT.
>> —Amen.

67

I love to tell the story of unseen things above,
Of JESUS and His glory, of JESUS and His love,
I love to tell the story, because I know 'tis true,
It satisfies my longings, as nothing else can do.

CHORUS.

I love to tell the story, 'twill be my theme in glory,
To tell the old, old story, of JESUS and His love.

I love to tell the story; more wonderful it seems
Than all the golden fancies of all our golden dreams;
I love to tell the story, it did so much for me!
And that is just the reason I tell it now to thee.—CHO.

I love to tell the story, 'tis pleasant to repeat
What seems, each time I tell it, more wonderfully sweet,
I love to tell the story; for some have never heard
The message of Salvation from GOD'S own Holy Word.—CHO.

I love to tell the story; for those who
  know it best,
Seem hungering and thirsting to hear it
  like the rest,
And when, in scenes of glory, I sing the
  new, new song,
'Twill be the old, old story, that I have
  loved so long.—Cho.—Amen.

68

Just as I am, without one plea,
But that Thy Blood was shed for me,
And that Thou bidd'st me come to Thee,
  O Lamb of God, I come!

Just as I am, and waiting not
To rid my soul of one dark blot,
To Thee, whose Blood can cleanse each [spot,
  O Lamb of God, I come!

Just as I am, though toss'd about
With many a conflict, many a doubt,
Fightings and fears within, without,
  O Lamb of God, I come!

Just as I am—poor, wretched, blind:
Sight, riches, healing of the mind,
Yea, all I need, in Thee to find,
  O Lamb of God, I come!

Just as I am, Thou wilt receive,
Wilt welcome, pardon, cleanse, relieve!
Because Thy promise I believe,
  O Lamb of God, I come!

Just as I am—Thy love unknown
Has broken every barrier down—
Now, to be Thine, yea, Thine alone,
  O Lamb of God, I come!

Just as I am, of that free love
The breadth, length, depth, and height
  to prove,

Here for a season, then above,
    O Lamb of God, I come!—Amen.

69

Jesu, Lover of my soul,
    Let me to Thy bosom fly,
While the waters nearer roll,
    While the tempest still is high.
Hide me, O my Saviour! hide,
    Till the storm of life is past:
Safe into the haven guide,
    O receive my soul at last!

Other refuge have I none,
    Hangs my helpless soul on Thee;
Leave—ah! leave me not alone,
    Still support and comfort me.
All my trust on Thee is stay'd,
    All my help from Thee I bring;
Cover my defenceless head
    With the shadow of Thy wing.

Thou, O Christ, art all I want:
    More than all in Thee I find:
Raise the fallen, cheer the faint,
    Heal the sick, and lead the blind;
Just and holy is Thy Name;
    I am all unrighteousness;
False and full of sin I am:
    Thou art full of truth and grace.

Plenteous grace with Thee is found,
    Grace to cover all my sin;
Let the healing streams abound,
    Make and keep me pure within.
Thou of life the fountain art,
    Freely let me take of Thee;
Spring Thou up within my heart:
    Rise to all eternity.—Amen.

70

Forty days and forty nights
Thou wast fasting in the wild;
Forty days and forty nights
Tempted, and yet undefiled.

Sunbeams scorching all the day;
Chilly dew-drops nightly shed:
Prowling beasts about Thy way;
Stones Thy pillow; earth Thy bed.

Shall not we Thy sorrow share,
Learn Thy discipline of pain,
Strive, like Thee, through fast and prayer,
Strength for after time to gain?

Then if Satan, vexing sore,
Flesh or spirit should assail,
Thou, his Vanquisher before,
Wilt not suffer us to fail.

So shall we have peace divine;
Holier gladness ours shall be;
Round us, too, shall Angels shine,
Such as ministered to Thee.

Keep, oh, keep us, SAVIOUR dear,
Ever constant by Thy side,
That with Thee we may appear
At the eternal Eastertide.—Amen.

71

When, His salvation bringing,
  To Zion JESUS came,
The children all stood singing
  Hosanna to His Name;
Nor did their zeal offend Him,
  But as He rode along
He let them still attend Him,
  And listened to their song.
      Hosanna to JESUS we'll sing.

And since the LORD retaineth
  His love for children still,
Though now as King He reigneth
  On Zion's heavenly hill,
We'll flock around His banner
  Who sits upon the Throne,
And cry aloud Hosanna
  To David's royal Son.
      Hosanna to JESUS, &c.

For should we fail proclaiming
  Our great REDEEMER'S praise,
The stones, our silence shaming,
  Would their hosannas raise.
But shall we only render
  The tribute of our words?
No: while our hearts are tender,
  They, too, shall be the LORD'S.
      Hosanna to JESUS, &c.—Amen.

72

Glory be to JESUS,
  Who, in bitter pains,
Poured for me the Life-Blood
  From His sacred veins..

Grace and life eternal
  In that Blood I find;
Blest be His compassion,
  Infinitely kind.

Blest through endless ages
  Be the precious stream,
Which from endless torments
  Did the world redeem.

Abel's blood for vengeance
  Pleaded to the skies;
But the Blood of JESUS
  For our pardon cries.

Oft as it is sprinkled
   On our guilty hearts,
Satan in confusion
   Terror-struck departs;
Oft as earth exulting
   Wafts its praise on high,
Angel hosts rejoicing
   Make their glad reply.
Lift ye then your voices;
   Swell the mighty flood;
Louder still and louder
   Praise the precious Blood.—Amen.

73

Angels, from the realms of glory
   Wing your flight o'er all the earth;
Ye who sang creation's story
   Now proclaim MESSIAH's birth!
     Come and worship—
Worship CHRIST, the new-born King!

Shepherds in the field abiding,
   Watching o'er your flocks by night,
GOD with man is now residing;
   Yonder shines the heavenly light.
     Come and worship—&c.

Saints before the altar bending,
   Watching long in hope and fear;
Suddenly the LORD, descending,
   In His temple shall appear.
     Come and worship—&c.—Amen.

74

Alleluia! Alleluia! Alleluia!
The strife is o'er, the battle done;
Now is the Victor's triumph won;
O let the song of praise be sung,
              Alleluia!

Death's mightiest powers have done their worst,
And JESUS hath His foes dispersed;
Let shouts of praise and joy outburst,
   Alleluia!

On the third morn He rose again
Glorious in majesty to reign;
O let us swell the joyous strain,
   Alleluia!

LORD, by the stripes which wounded Thee,
From death's dread sting Thy servants free,
That we may live and sing to Thee,
   Alleluia!—Amen.

75

Come, Thou long-expected JESUS,
 Born to set Thy people free,
From our sins and fears release us,
 Let us find our rest in Thee.

Israel's strength and consolation,
 Hope of all the earth Thou art,
Dear desire of every nation,
 Joy of every longing heart.

Born Thy people to deliver,
 Born a child and yet a King;
Born to reign in us for ever,
 Now Thy gracious kingdom bring.

By Thine own eternal SPIRIT
 Rule in all our hearts alone;
By Thine all-sufficient merit
 Raise us to Thy glorious Throne.
     —Amen.

76

Jesus, we love to meet
  On this Thy holy day;
We worship round Thy seat
  On this Thy holy day.
Thou tender, Heavenly Friend,
To Thee our prayers ascend,
O'er our young spirits bend,
  On this Thy holy day.

We dare not trifle now,
  On this Thy holy day;
In silent awe we bow,
  On this Thy holy day.
Check every wandering thought,
And let us all be taught
To serve Thee as we ought,
  On this Thy holy day.

We listen to Thy Word,
  On this Thy holy day:
Bless all that we have heard
  On this Thy holy day.
Go with us when we part,
And to each youthful heart
Thy saving grace impart,
  On this Thy holy day.—Amen.

77

Blest are the pure in heart,
  For they shall see our God;
The secret of the Lord is theirs,
  Their soul is Christ's abode.

The Lord, who left the Heavens,
  Our life and peace to bring.
To dwell in lowliness with men,
  Their Pattern and their King,

He to the lowly soul
  Doth still Himself impart,
And for His dwelling and His throne
  Chooseth the pure in heart.

Lord, we Thy Presence seek;
  May ours this blessing be:
Give us a pure and lowly heart,
  A temple meet for Thee.—Amen.

78

Soldiers of Christ, arise,
  And put your armour on,
Strong in the strength which God sup-
  Through His Eternal Son.   [plies

Strong in the Lord of hosts,
  And in His mighty power;
Who in the strength of Jesus trusts
  Is more than conqueror.

Stand then in His great might,
  With all His strength endued;
And take, to arm you for the fight,
  The panoply of God.

From strength to strength go on,
  Wrestle, and fight, and pray;
Tread all the powers of darkness down,
  And win the well-fought day;

That having all things done,
  And all your conflicts past,
Ye may obtain, through Christ alone,
  A crown of joy at last.

Jesu, Eternal Son,
  We praise Thee and adore,
Who art with God the Father One,
  And Spirit, evermore.—Amen.

79

Sweet SAVIOUR, bless us ere we go;
   Thy Word into our minds instil,
And make our lukewarm hearts to glow
   With lowly love and fervent will.
Through life's long day and death's dark [night,
O gentle JESUS, be our Light.

The day is gone, its hours have run,
   And Thou hast taken count of all,
The scanty triumphs grace hath won,
   The broken vow, the frequent fall.
Through life's long day and death's dark [night,
O gentle JESUS, be our Light.

Grant us, dear LORD, from evil ways
   True absolution and release;
And bless us, more than in past days,
   With purity and inward peace.
Through life's long day and death's dark [night.
O gentle JESUS, be our Light.

Do more than pardon; give us joy,
   Sweet fear, and sober liberty,
And simple hearts without alloy
   That only long to be like Thee.
Through life's long day and death's dark [night,
O gentle JESUS, be our Light.

For all we love, the poor, the sad,
   The sinful, unto Thee we call;
O let Thy mercy make us glad:
   Thou art our JESUS, and our All.
Through life's long day and death's dark [night,
O gentle JESUS, be our Light.
                —Amen.

80

And now, O FATHER, mindful of the love
　That bought us, once for all, on Calvary's Tree,
And having with us Him that pleads above,
　We here present, we here spread forth to Thee
That only Offering perfect in Thine eyes.
The one true, pure, immortal Sacrifice.

Look, FATHER, look on His Anointed Face,
　And only look on us as found in Him;
Look not on our misusings of Thy grace,
　Our prayer so languid, and our faith so dim;
For lo! between our sins and their reward
We set the Passion of Thy SON our LORD.

And then for those, our dearest and our best,
　By this prevailing Presence we appeal;
O fold them closer to Thy mercy's breast,
　O do Thine utmost for their soul's true weal;
From tainting mischief keep them white and clear,
And crown Thy gifts with strength to persevere.

And so we come; O draw us to Thy feet,
　Most patient Saviour, Who canst love us still;
And by this Food, so awful and so sweet,
　Deliver us from every touch of ill:

In Thine own service make us glad and
    free,
And grant us never more to part with
    Thee.   —Amen.

81

FATHER of all, from land and sea
The nations sing, "Thine, LORD, are we,
Countless in number, but in Thee
    May we be one."

O SON of GOD, Whose love so free
For men did make Thee Man to be,
United to our GOD in Thee
    May we be one.

Thou, LORD, didst once for all atone;
Thee may both Jew and Gentile own
Of their two walls the Corner Stone,
    Making them one.

In Thee we are GOD's Israel,
Thou art the world's Emmanuel,
In Thee the saints for ever dwell,
    Millions, but one.

Thou art the Fountain of all good,
Cleansing with Thy most precious Blood,
And feeding us with Angels' Food,
    Making us one.

Join high and low, join young and old
In love that never waxes cold;
Under one Shepherd, in one Fold,
    Make us all one.

O SPIRIT blest, Who from above
Cam'st gently gliding like a dove,
Calm all our strife, give faith and love·
    O make us one.

O TRINITY in UNITY,
ONE only GOD, in Persons THREE,
Dwell ever in our hearts; like Thee
    May we be one.

So, when the world shall pass away,
May we awake with joy and say,
"Now in the bliss of endless day
    We all are one." —Amen.

82

All glory, laud, and honour
  To Thee, Redeemer, King,
To Whom the lips of children
  Made sweet Hosannas ring!

Thou art the King of Israel,
  Thou, David's Royal Son,
Who in the LORD's Name comest,
  The King and Blessed One.
    All glory, &c.

The company of Angels
  Are praising Thee on high,
And mortal men and all things
  Created make reply.
    All glory, &c.

The people of the Hebrews
  With palms before Thee went;
Our praise and prayer and anthems
  Before Thee we present.
    All glory, &c.

To Thee, before Thy Passion,
  They sang their hymns of praise;
To Thee, now high exalted,
  Our melody we raise.
    All glory, &c.

Thou didst accept their praises,
  Accept the prayers we bring,
Who in all good delightest,
  Thou good and gracious King.
          All glory, &c.—Amen.

83

Hear Thy children, gentle JESUS,
  While we breathe our evening prayer;
Save us from all harm and danger,
  Take us 'neath Thy sheltering care.

Shield us from the wiles of Satan,
  From the perils of this night;
Safely may our guardian Angels
  Keep us in their watchful sight.

Gentle JESUS! look in pity
  From Thy glorious Throne above;
Though we sleep, Thy Heart is wakeful,
  Still for us It beats with love.

Shades of evening fast are falling,
  Day is fading into gloom;
When our earthly life is ended,
  Lead Thy ransomed children home.

Gentle JESUS! hear Thy children
  When they sing their hymns to Thee;
Who, with FATHER and with SPIRIT,
  Art ONE GOD eternally.—Amen.

84

When our heads are bowed with woe,
When our bitter tears o'erflow,
When we mourn the lost, the dear,
JESU, Son of Mary, hear.

Thou our throbbing flesh hast worn,
Thou our mortal griefs hast borne,
Thou hast shed the human tear;
JESU, Son of Mary, hear.

When the solemn death-bell tolls
For our own departing souls,
When our final doom is near,
JESU, Son of Mary, hear.

Thou hast bowed the dying head,
Thou the blood of life hast shed,
Thou hast filled a mortal bier;
JESU, Son of Mary, hear.

When the heart is sad within
With the thought of all its sin,
When the spirit shrinks with fear,
JESU, Son of Mary, hear.

Thou the shame, the grief, hast known,
Though the sins were not Thine own;
Thou hast deigned their load to bear:
JESU, Son of Mary, hear.—Amen.

85

See the destined day arise!
See, a willing Sacrifice,
JESUS, to redeem our loss,
Hangs upon the shameful Cross!

JESU, who but Thou had borne,
Lifted on that Tree of scorn,
Every pang and bitter throe,
Finishing Thy life of woe?

Who but Thou had dared to drain,
Steeped in gall, the cup of pain,
And with tender Body bear
Thorns, and nails, and piercing spear?

Thence the cleansing Water flowed,
Mingled from Thy Side with Blood;
Sign to all attesting eyes
Of the finished Sacrifice.

Holy JESU, grant us grace
In that Sacrifice to place
All our trust for life renewed,
Pardoned sin, and promised good.
—Amen.

86

O come and mourn with me awhile;
O come ye to the Saviour's side;
O come, together let us mourn;
JESUS, our LORD, is crucified.

Have we no tears to shed for Him,
While soldiers scoff and Jews deride?
Ah! look how patiently He hangs;
JESUS, our LORD, is crucified.

How fast His Hands and Feet are nailed;
His Throat with parching thirst is dried;
His failing Eyes are dimmed with Blood;
JESUS, our Lord, is crucified.

Seven times He spake, seven Words of
    love;
And all three hours His silence cried
For mercy on the souls of men;
JESUS, our LORD, is crucified.

Come, let us stand beneath the Cross;
So may the Blood from out His Side
Fall gently on us drop by drop;
JESUS, our LORD, is crucified.

A broken heart, a fount of tears,
Ask, and they will not be denied;
LORD JESUS, may we love and weep,
Since Thou for us art crucified.—Amen.

87

Sweet the moments, rich in blessing,
  Which before the Cross I spend,
Life, and health, and peace possessing
  From the sinner's dying Friend.

Here I rest, for ever viewing
  Mercy poured in streams of Blood;
Precious drops, my soul bedewing,
  Plead and claim my peace with GOD.

Truly blessed is the station,
  Low before His Cross to lie,
Whilst I see Divine compassion
  Beaming in His languid Eye.

LORD, in ceaseless contemplation
  Fix my thankful heart on Thee,
Till I taste Thy full salvation,
  And Thine unveiled glory see.—Amen.

88

O sacred Head, surrounded
  By crown of piercing thorn!
O bleeding Head, so wounded,
  Reviled, and put to scorn!
Death's pallid hue comes o'er Thee,
  The glow of life decays,
Yet Angel-hosts adore Thee,
  And tremble as they gaze.

I see Thy strength and vigour
  All fading in the strife,
And death with cruel rigour
  Bereaving Thee of life;
O agony and dying!
  O love to sinners free!
JESU, all grace supplying,
  O turn Thy Face on me.

In this Thy bitter Passion,
  Good Shepherd, think of me
With Thy most sweet compassion,
  Unworthy though I be:
Beneath Thy Cross abiding
  For ever would I rest,
In Thy dear love confiding,
  And with Thy presence blest.—Amen.

89

Far from my heavenly home,
  Far from my FATHER's breast,
Fainting I cry, "Blest SPIRIT, come,
  And speed me to my rest."

My spirit homeward turns,
  And fain would thither flee;
My heart, O Sion, droops and yearns,
  When I remember thee.

To thee, to thee, I press,
  A dark and toilsome road;
When shall I pass the wilderness,
  And reach the Saints' abode?

GOD of my life, be near;
  On Thee my hopes I cast;
O guide me through the desert here,
  And bring me home at last.—Amen.

90

Come, ye faithful, raise the strain
  Of triumphant gladness;
GOD hath brought His Israel
  Into joy from sadness;
Loosed from Pharaoh's bitter yoke
  Jacob's sons and daughters;
Led them with unmoistened foot
  Through the Red Sea waters.

'Tis the spring of souls to-day;
　Christ hath burst His prison,
And from three days' sleep in death
　As a sun hath risen;
All the winter of our sins,
　Long and dark, is flying
From His Light, to Whom we give
　Laud and praise undying.

Now the Queen of seasons, bright
　With the Day of splendour,
With the royal Feast of feasts,
　Comes its joy to render;
Comes to glad Jerusalem,
　Who with true affection
Welcomes in unwearied strains
　Jesu's Resurrection.

Alleluia now we cry
　To our King Immortal,
Who triumphant burst the bars
　Of the tomb's dark portal;
Alleluia, with the Son
　God the Father praising;
Alleluia yet again
　To the Spirit raising.—Amen.

91

Ride on! ride on in majesty!
Hark! all the tribes Hosanna cry;
O Saviour meek, pursue Thy road
With palms and scattered garments
　　　strowed.

Ride on! ride on in majesty!
In lowly pomp ride on to die;
O Christ, Thy triumph now begin
O'er captive death and conquered sin.

Ride on! ride on in majesty!
The Angel armies of the sky
Look down with sad and wondering eyes
To see the approaching Sacrifice.

Ride on! ride on in majesty!
The last and fiercest strife is nigh:
The FATHER on His sapphire Throne
Awaits His own Anointed SON.

Ride on! ride on in majesty!
In lowly pomp ride on to die;
Bow Thy meek Head to mortal pain,
Then take, O GOD, Thy power, and reign.
—Amen.

92

At the Cross her station keeping
Stood the mournful Mother weeping,
   Where He hung, the dying LORD;
For her soul of joy bereaved,
Bowed with anguish, deeply grieved,
   Felt the sharp and piercing sword.

Oh, how sad and sore distressed
Now was she, that Mother blessed
   Of the sole-begotten One;
Deep the woe of her affliction,
When she saw the Crucifixion
   Of her ever-glorious Son.

Who, on CHRIST's dear Mother gazing
Pierced by anguish so amazing,
   Born of woman, would not weep?
Who, on CHRIST's dear Mother thinking,
Such a cup of sorrow drinking,
   Would not share her sorrow deep?

For His people's sins chastised,
She beheld her Son despised, [twined;
   Scourged, and crowned with thorns en-
Saw Him then from judgment taken,
And in death by all forsaken,
   Till His Spirit He resigned.

Jesu, may her deep devotion
Stir in me the same emotion,
   Fount of love, Redeemer kind,
That my heart fresh ardour gaining,
And a purer love attaining,
   May with Thee acceptance find.
                     —Amen.

93

There is a green hill far away,
   Without a city wall,
Where the dear LORD was crucified,
   Who died to save us all.

We may not know, we cannot tell,
   What pains He had to bear;
But we believe it was for us
   He hung and suffered there.

He died that we might be forgiven,
   He died to make us good,
That we might go at last to Heaven,
   Saved by His precious Blood.

There was no other good enough
   To pay the price of sin;
He only could unlock the gate
   Of Heaven, and let us in.

Oh, dearly, dearly has He loved!
   And we must love Him too,
And trust in His redeeming Blood,
   And try His works to do.—Amen.

94

Easter flowers are blooming bright,
Easter skies pour radiant light,
CHRIST our Lord is risen in might,
   Glory in the highest.

Angels carolled this sweet lay,
When in manger rude He lay;
Now once more cast grief away,
   Glory in the highest.

He, then born to grief and pain,
Now to glory born again,
Calleth forth our gladdest strain,
   Glory in the highest,

As He riseth, rise we too,
Tune we heart and voice anew,
Offering homage glad and true,
   Glory in the highest.—Amen.

95

Faithful Cross, above all others,
   One and only noble Tree,
None in foliage, none in blossom,
   None in fruit thy peer may be;
Sweetest wood, and sweetest iron;
   Sweetest weight is hung on thee.

Bend, O lofty tree, thy branches,
   Thy too rigid sinews bend;
And awhile the stubborn hardness,
   Which thy birth bestowed, suspend;
And the limbs of Heaven's High Monarch
   Gently on thine arms extend.

Thou alone was counted worthy
   This world's Ransom to sustain,
That a shipwrecked race forever

Might a port of refuge gain,
With the Sacred Blood anointed
Of the Lamb for sinners slain.

96

Hail! Festal Day! for evermore adored!
Wherein God conquered Hell and upward soared.
  (Repeat in Chorus.)

See the world's beauty, budding forth anew
Shews with the Lord, His gifts returning too!
  Hail! Festal Day.

The earth with flowers is decked—the sky serene;
The Heavenly Portals glow with brighter sheen,
  Hail! Festal Day.

The greenwood leaves—the flowering meadows tell
Of Christ, triumphant over gloomy Hell.
  Hail! Festal Day.

The power of Satan crushed, He seeks the skies;
From earth, light, stars and ocean anthems rise!
  Hail! Festal Day.

The Crucified reigns God for evermore,
Their Maker all created things adore.
  Hail! Festal Day.

Christ Who didst fashion man and hast rewon
The Eternal, Father's sole-begotten Son.
  Hail! Festal Day.

When Death and Hell the human race
    o'er-ran,
Then, man to save, becamest Man.
    Hail! Festal Day.—Amen.

97

Golden harps are sounding,
    Angel voices sing,
Pearly gates are opened,
    Opened for the King;
Jesus, King of Glory,
    Jesus, King of Love,
Is gone up in triumph
    To His throne above.

    All His work is ended,
      Joyfully we sing;
    Jesus hath ascended!
      Glory to our King!

He who came to save us,
    He who bled and died,
Now is crowned with glory,
    At His Father's Side.
Never more to suffer,
    Never more to die;
Jesus, King of Glory,
    Is gone up on high!
    All His work, &c.

Praying for His children
    In that blessed place,
Calling them to glory,
    Sending them His grace;
His bright home preparing,
    Faithful ones, for you;
Jesus ever liveth,
    Ever loveth too.
    All His work, &c.—Amen.

98

Behold the LAMB of GOD!
O Thou for sinners slain,
Let it not be in vain
  That Thou hast died;
Thee for my SAVIOUR let me take,
My only refuge let me make
  Thy pierced Side.

Behold the LAMB of GOD!
Into the sacred flood
Of Thy most precious Blood
  My soul I cast:
Wash me and make me clean within,
And keep me pure from every sin,
  Till life be past.

Behold the LAMB of GOD!
All hail, Incarnate WORD,
Thou everlasting LORD,
  SAVIOUR most Blest;
Fill us with love that never faints,
Grant us with all Thy blessed Saints
  Eternal rest.

Behold the LAMB of GOD!
Worthy is He alone
To sit upon the Throne
  Of GOD above;
One with the Ancient of all days,
One with the Comforter in praise,
  All Light and Love.—Amen.

99

JESUS CHRIST is risen to-day, Alleluia!
Our triumphant holy-day, Alleluia!
Who did once upon the Cross, Alleluia!
Suffer to redeem our loss, Alleluia!

Hymns of praise then let us sing, Alleluia!
Unto CHRIST, our Heavenly King,
       Alleluia!
Who endured the Cross and grave,
       Alleluia!
Sinners to redeem and save, Alleluia!

But the pain which He endured, Alleluia!
Our salvation has procured; Alleluia!
Now above the sky He's King, Alleluia!
Where the Angels ever sing— Alleluia!
       —Amen.

100

Who is this, so weak and helpless,
 Child of lowly Hebrew maid,
Rudely in a stable sheltered,
 Coldly in a manger laid?
'Tis the LORD of all creation,
 Who this wondrous path hath trod;
He is GOD from everlasting,
 And to everlasting, GOD.

Who is this—a Man of Sorrows,
 Walking sadly life's hard way,
Homeless, weary, sighing, weeping
 Over sin and Satan's sway?
'Tis our GOD, our glorious SAVIOUR,
 Who above the starry sky
Now for us a place prepareth,
 Where no tear can dim the eye.

Who is this? behold Him shedding
 Drops of Blood upon the ground.
Who is this? despised, rejected,
 Mocked, insulted, beaten, bound?
'Tis our GOD, Who gifts and graces
 On His Church now poureth down;
Who shall smite in holy vengeance
 All His foes beneath His Throne.

Who is this that hangeth dying
While the rude world scoffs and scorns?
  Numbered with the malefactors,
  Torn with nails and crowned with
      thorns?
'Tis the GOD Who ever liveth
  'Mid the shining ones on high,
In the glorious golden city
  Reigning everlastingly.—Amen.

101

Hail the day that sees Him rise Alleluia!
To His Throne above the skies; Alleluia!
CHRIST, the Lamb for sinners given,
              Alleluia!
Enters now the highest Heaven. Alleluia!

There for Him high triumph waits;
              Alleluia!
Lift your heads, eternal gates; Alleluia!
He hath conquered death and sin;
              Alleluia!
Take the King of Glory in. Alleluia!

Lo! the Heaven its LORD receives,
              Alleluia!
Yet He loves the earth He leaves;
              Alleluia!
Though returning to His Throne
              Alleluia!
Still He calls mankind His own.
              Alleluia!

See! He lifts His Hands above; Alleluia!
See! He shows the prints of love;
              Alleluia!
Hark! His gracious Lips bestow
              Alleluia!
Blessings on His Church below. Alleluia!

Still for us He intercedes,   Alleluia!
His prevailing death He pleads, Alleluia!
Near Himself prepares our place,
                        Alleluia!
He the first-fruits of our race. Alleluia!

Lord, though parted from our sight
                        Alleluia!
Far above the starry height,   Alleluia!
Grant our hearts may thither rise,
                        Alleluia!
Seeking Thee above the skies. Alleluia!
                          —Amen.

102

O Jesus Christ remember,
  When Thou shalt come again
Upon the clouds of Heaven,
  With all Thy shining train;

When every eye shall see Thee
  In Deity revealed,
Who now upon this Altar
  In silence art concealed;

Remember then, O Saviour,
  I supplicate of Thee,
That here I bowed before Thee
  Upon my bended knee.

That here I owned Thy Presence,
  And did not Thee deny,
And glorified Thy Greatness,
  Though hid from human eye.

Accept, Divine Redeemer,
  The homage of my praise;
Be Thou the Light and Honor,
  And Glory of my days.

Be Thou my Consolation
  When death is drawing nigh;
Be Thou my only Treasure
  Through all eternity.—Amen.

103

At the LAMB's high feast we sing
Praise to our victorious King,
Who hath washed us in the tide
Flowing from His pierced Side;
Praise we Him, Whose love divine
Gives His Sacred Blood for wine,
Gives His Body for the feast,
CHRIST the Victim, CHRIST the Priest.

Where the Paschal blood is poured,
Death's dark Angel sheathes his sword;
Israel's hosts triumphant go
Through the wave that drowns the foe.
Praise we CHRIST, Whose Blood was shed,
Paschal Victim, Paschal Bread;
With sincerity and love
Eat we Manna from above.

Mighty Victim from the sky,
Hell's fierce powers beneath Thee lie;
Thou hast conquered in the fight,
Thou hast brought us life and light;
Now no more can death appal,
Now no more the grave enthral;
Thou hast opened Paradise,
And in Thee Thy saints shall rise.

Easter triumph, Easter joy,
Sin alone can this destroy;
From sin's power do Thou set free
Souls new-born, O LORD, in Thee.
Hymns of glory and of praise,
Risen LORD, to Thee we raise;
Holy FATHER, praise to Thee,
With the SPIRIT, ever be.—Amen.

104

THE STORY OF THE CROSS.

"Is it nothing to you, all ye that pass by? Behold and see, if there be any sorrow like unto My sorrow."—Lam. i: 12.

THE QUESTION.

In His own raiment clad,
  With His Blood dyed;
Women walk sorrowing
  By His side.
Heavy that Cross to Him—
  Weary the weight;
One who will help Him waits
  At the gate.

See! they are travelling
  On the same road—
Simon is sharing with
  Him the load.

Oh! whither wandering
  Bear they that Tree?
He who first carries it—
  Who is He?

THE ANSWER.

Follow to Calvary—
  Tread where He trod—
He Who forever was
  Son of God.
You who would love Him, stand,
  Gaze at His Face:
Tarry awhile on your
  Earthly race.
Let not the crucified
  Call thee in vain;
See how He hangs there
  In bitter pain.

Is there no beauty to
   You who pass by
In that lone Figure which
   Marks the sky?

THE STORY OF THE CROSS.

On the Cross lifted,
   Thy Face I scan—
Bearing that Cross for me,
   Son of Man.

Thorns form Thy diadem,
   Rough wood Thy Throne;
For us Thy Blood is shed—
   Us alone.

No pillow under Thee
   To rest Thy Head—
Only the splintered Cross
   Is Thy Bed.

Nails pierce Thy Hands and Feet,
   Thy Side the spear;
No voice is nigh, to say
   Help is near.

Shadows of midnight fall,
   Though it is day—
Thy friends and kinsfolk stand
   Far away.

Loud is Thy bitter cry;
   Sunk on Thy Breast
Hangeth Thy bleeding Head
   Without rest.

Loud scoffs the dying thief,
   Who mocks at Thee—
Can it, my Saviour, be
   All for me?

Gazing afar from Thee,
  Silent and lone,
Stand those few weepers Thou
  Callest Thine Own.

I see Thy title, LORD,
  Inscribed above:
"JESUS OF NAZARETH,"
  King of Love!

What, O my SAVIOUR,
  Here didst Thou See,
That made Thee suffer and
  Die for me?

THE APPEAL FROM THE CROSS.

Child of My grief and pain,
  Watched by My love,
I came to call thee to
  Realms above.

I saw thee wandering
  Far off from Me;
In love I seek for thee—
  Do not flee.

For thee My Blood I shed—
  For Thee alone;
I came to purchase thee
  For Mine own.

Weep not for My grief,
  Child of My love;
Strive to be with Me in
  Heaven above.

OUR CRY TO JESUS.

Oh! I will follow Thee,
  Star of my soul,
Through the deep shades of life,
  To the goal.

Yes, let Thy Cross be borne
    Each day by me—
Mind not how heavy, if
    But with Thee.

LORD, if Thou only wilt
    Make me Thine own,
Give no companion save
    Thee alone.

Grant through each day of life
    To stand by Thee,
With Thee when morning breaks,
    Ever to be.—Amen.

105

JESUS, high in glory,
    Lend a listening ear;
When we bow before Thee,
    Children's praises hear.

Though Thou art so holy,
    Heaven's Almighty King,
Thou wilt stoop to listen,
    When Thy praise we sing.

We are little children,
    Weak and apt to stray;
SAVIOUR, guide and keep us
    In the heavenly way.

Save us, LORD, from sinning;
    Watch us day by day;
Help us now to love Thee;
    Take our sins away:

Then, when Thou dost call us
    To our heavenly home,
We shall gladly answer,
    SAVIOUR, LORD, we come.—Amen.

106

Our Lord, He was a carpenter,
  Who wrought with saw and plane,
And did in Naz'reth, thirty years,
  A working man remain:
But while He wrought, the heart and
    thought
  Of our most loving Lord
Were ever how to build His Church
  And preach the glorious Word.
    Then, working men, be brave, be
        strong,
      To serve the Lord alway;
    Remember what Augustine said:
      "To labour is to pray."

Saint Peter was a fisherman,
  Who toiled upon the wave:
"Henceforth shalt thou catch men,"
    said Christ,
  "And sinful souls shalt save."
"Thou art a rock, and I will build
  My holy Church on thee;
The keys of Heaven thou shalt hold,
  Come, follow after me."
    Then, working men, etc.

Saint Paul, he was a tentmaker,
  And, working at his trade
With them that were of self-same craft
  For Christ he converts made.
"These hands," he said, "have ministered
  To my necessity;"
And herein gathered his reward,—
  He made the gospel free.
    Then, working men, etc.

The good physician Luke, whose praise
    Through all the churches rolls,
Like his great Master, toiled to save
    Men's bodies and men's souls.
From him we learn those songs divine,
    Which men and angels too,
Sing day by day. O what weak man
    With zeal for GOD may do!
        Then, working men, etc.

A rich young ruler came to CHRIST,
    "LORD I will follow Thee;
The ten commandments I have kept,
    What lacketh yet to me?"
"Give all thy wealth to feed the poor,
    And thou shalt win the crown."
Alas! he could not rise to that,
    His riches held him down.
        Then, working men, etc.

GOD's saints in every age and clime,
    All in their several ways,
With heart and hand, in life and death,
    Have labored for His praise:
And we too, brothers, wheresoe'er
    Our humble lot may lie,
Can work for Him, who was content
    For us to work—and die!
        Then, working men, etc.—Amen.

107

The KING of love my Shepherd is,
    Whose goodness faileth never;
I nothing lack if I am His
    And He is mine for ever.

Where streams of living water flow
    My ransomed soul He leadeth,
And, where the verdant pastures grow,
    With food celestial feedeth.

Perverse and foolish oft I strayed,
    But yet in love He sought me,
And on His Shoulder gently laid,
    And home, rejoicing, brought me.

In death's dark vale I fear no ill
    With Thee, dear LORD, beside me;
Thy rod and staff my comfort still,
    Thy Cross before to guide me.

Thou spread'st a Table in my sight,
    Thy Unction grace bestoweth,
And oh! what transport of delight
    From Thy pure Chalice floweth.

And so through all the length of days
    Thy goodness faileth never;
Good Shepherd, may I sing Thy praise
    Within Thy house for ever.—Amen.

108

Rejoice, ye pure in heart!
Rejoice! give thanks and sing;
Your festal banner wave on high,
    The Cross of CHRIST, your King.

Bright youth and snow-crowned age,
    Strong men and maidens meek,
Raise high your free exulting song,
    GOD's wondrous praises speak.

Yes, onward, onward still,
    With hymn, and chant, and song,
Through gate, and porch, and columned
    The hallowed pathways throng. [aisle,

With all the Angel choirs,
    With all the saints on earth,
Pour out the strains of joy and bliss,
    True rapture, noblest mirth.

  Your clear Hosannas raise,
   And Allelujas loud;
Whilst answering echoes upward float,
   Like wreaths of incense cloud.

  With voice as full and strong
   As ocean's surging praise,
Send forth the hymns our fathers loved,
   The psalms of ancient days.

  Yes, on through life's long path,
   Still chanting as ye go,
From youth to age, by night and day,
   In gladness and in woe.

  Still lift your standard high,
   Still march in firm array,
As warriors through the darkness toil
   Till dawns the golden day.

  At last the march shall end,
   The wearied ones shall rest,
The pilgrims find their FATHER'S house,
   Jerusalem the blest.

  Then on, ye pure in heart,
   Rejoice, give thanks, and sing;
Your festal banner wave on high,
   The Cross of CHRIST, your King.

  Praise Him Who reigns on high,
   The LORD Whom we adore,
The FATHER, SON, and HOLY GHOST
   One GOD for evermore.—Amen.

109

Through the night of doubt and sorrow
  Onward goes the pilgrim band,
Singing songs of expectation,
  Marching to the Promised Land.

Clear before us through the darkness
   Gleams and burns the guiding light.
Brother clasps the hand of brother,
   Stepping fearless through the night.

One the light of GOD's own presence
   O'er His ransomed people shed,
Chasing far the gloom and terror,
   Brightening all the path we tread:

One the object of our journey,
   One the faith which never tires,
One the earnest looking forward,
   One the hope our GOD inspires:

One the strain that lips of thousands
   Lift as from the heart of one;
One the conflict, one the peril,
   One the march in GOD begun:

One the gladness of rejoicing
   On the far eternal shore,
Where the ONE ALMIGHTY FATHER
   Reigns in love for evermore.

Onward therefore, pilgrim brothers,
   Onward with the Cross our aid!
Bear its shame, and fight its battle,
   Till we rest beneath its shade.

Soon shall come the great awaking,
   Soon the rending of the tomb;
Then the scattering of all shadows,
   And the end of toil and gloom.—Amen.

110

There's a Friend for little children
   Above the bright blue sky,
A Friend Who never changes,
   Whose love will never die;

Our earthly friends may fail us,
    And change with changing years
This Friend is always worthy
Of that dear Name He bears.

There's a rest for little children
    Above the bright blue sky,
Who love the Blessed SAVIOUR,
    And to the FATHER cry;
A rest from every turmoil,
    From sin and sorrow free,
Where every little pilgrim
    Shall rest eternally.

There's a home for little children
    Above the bright blue sky,
Where JESUS reigns in glory,
    A home of peace and joy;
No home on earth is like it,
    Nor can with it compare;
For every one is happy,
    Nor could be happier, there.

There's a crown for little children
    Above the bright blue sky,
And all who look for JESUS
    Shall wear it by-and-by:
A crown of brightest glory,
    Which He will then bestow
On those who found His favour,
    And loved His Name below.

There's a song for little children
    Above the bright blue sky,
A song that will not weary,
    Though sung continually;
A song which even Angels
    Can never, never sing:
They know not CHRIST as SAVIOUR,
    But worship Him as King.

There's a robe for little children
   Above the bright blue sky;
And a harp of sweetest music,
   And palms of victory.
All, all above is treasured,
   And found in CHRIST alone;
LORD, grant Thy little children
   May know Thee as their own.—Amen

111

The Church's one foundation
   Is JESUS CHRIST her LORD;
She is His new creation
   By Water and the Word.
From Heaven He came and sought her
   To be His holy Bride;
With His own Blood He bought her,
   And for her life He died.

Elect from every nation,
   Yet one o'er all the earth,
Her charter of salvation
   One LORD, one Faith, one Birth,
One Holy Name she blesses,
   Partakes one Holy Food,
And to one hope she presses
   With every grace endued.

Though with a scornful wonder
   Men see her sore opprest,
By schisms rent asunder,
   By heresies distrest,
Yet saints their watch are keeping,
   Their cry goes up, "How long?"
And soon the night of weeping
   Shall be the morn of song.

Mid toil and tribulation,
   And tumult of her war,
She waits the consummation
   Of peace for evermore:

Till with the vision glorious
   Her longing eyes are blest,
And the great Church victorious
   Shall be the Church at rest.

Yet she on earth hath union
   With GOD the THREE in ONE,
And mystic sweet communion
   With those whose rest is won;
Oh, happy ones and holy!
   LORD, give us grace that we,
Like them, the meek and lowly,
   On high may dwell with Thee.
                —Amen.

112

Onward, Christian soldiers,
   Marching as to war,
With the Cross of JESUS
   Going on before;
CHRIST, the Royal Master,
   Leads against the foe;
Forward into battle
   See His banners go.
       Onward, Christian soldiers, &c.

At the sign of triumph
   Satan's host doth flee;
On then, Christian soldiers,
   On to victory;
Hell's foundations quiver
   At the shout of praise,
Brothers, lift your voices,
   Loud your anthems raise.
       Onward, Christian soldiers, &c.

Like a mighty army
   Moves the Church of GOD;
Brothers, we are treading
   Where the saints have trod;

We are not divided,
  All one body we,
One in hope and doctrine,
  One in charity.
    Onward, Christian soldiers, &c.

Crowns and thrones may perish,
  Kingdoms rise and wane,
But the Church of JESUS
  Constant will remain;
Gates of hell can never
  'Gainst that Church prevail:
We have CHRIST's own promise,
  And that cannot fail.
    Onward, Christian soldiers, &c.

Onward, then, ye people,
  Join our happy throng,
Blend with ours your voices
  In the triumph song:
Glory, laud, and honour
  Unto CHRIST the King,
This through countless ages
  Men and angels sing.
    Onward, Christian soldiers, &c.
        —Amen.

113

Alleluia! Alleluia! Alleluia!
O sons and daughters, let us sing!
The King of Heaven, the glorious King,
O'er death to-day rose triumphing.
    Alleluia!

That Sunday morn at break of day,
The faithful women went their way
To seek the tomb where JESUS lay.
    Alleluia!

An Angel clad in white they see,
Who sat, and spake unto the three,
"Your LORD doth go to Galilee."
     Alleluia!

That night the apostles met in fear,
Amidst them came their LORD most dear,
And said, "My peace be on all here."
     Alleluia!

When Thomas first the tidings heard,
How they had seen the risen LORD,
He doubted the disciples' word.
     Alleluia!

"My pierced Side, O Thomas, see;
My Hands, My Feet, I show to Thee;
Nor faithless, but believing be."
     Alleluia!

No longer Thomas then denied,
He saw the Feet, the Hands, the Side;
"Thou art my LORD and GOD," he cried.
     Alleluia!

How blest are they who have not seen,
And yet whose faith hath constant been;
For they eternal life shall win.
     Alleluia!

On this most holy day of days,
To GOD your hearts and voices raise,
In laud, and jubilee, and praise.
     Alleluia!—Amen.

114

HOLY GHOST, come down upon Thy children,
 Give us grace and make us Thine;
Thy tender fires within us kindle,
 Blessed SPIRIT! DOVE Divine!

For all within us good and holy
  Is from Thee, Thy precious gift;
In all our joys, in all our sorrows,
  Wistful hearts to Thee we lift.
    HOLY GHOST, &c.

O we have grieved Thee, Gracious SPIRIT!
  Wayward, wanton, cold are we;
And still our sins, new every morning,
  Never yet have wearied Thee.
    HOLY GHOST, &c.

Now, if our hearts do not deceive us,
  We would take Thee for our LORD;
O dearest SPIRIT! make us faithful
  To Thy least and lightest word.
    HOLY GHOST, &c.—Amen.

115

Our blest Redeemer, ere He breathed
  His tender last farewell,
A Guide, a Comforter, bequeathed
  With us to dwell.

He came sweet influence to impart,
  A gracious willing Guest,
While He can find one humble heart
  Wherein to rest.

And His that gentle Voice we hear,
  Soft as the breath of even,
That checks each fault, that calms each fear,
  And speaks of heaven.

And every virtue we possess,
  And every conquest won,
And every thought of holiness,
  Are His alone.

Spirit of purity and grace,
   Our weakness, pitying, see;
Oh, make our hearts Thy dwelling-place,
   And worthier Thee!—Amen.

116

A rhyme, a rhyme, for Easter time
   Come sing with mirth and glee;
Come youth and age, with sire and sage
   And join in harmony!
For Christ hath burst His prison gate,
   Whose bars before Him fell.
Aloft He fares and with Him bears
   The keys of death and Hell.

No powers of night can keep His soul
   Its prison bourns within;
Corruption foul can ne'er control
   His form unstained by sin.
His three days o'er, He comes once more
   To tread the hallowed sod
By Sion's gate, where hellish hate
   Had slain the Son of God.

But not alone doth Jesus speed;
   A throng of spirits bright
Away to earth with Him proceed,
   As trophies of His might.
Around doth press the saintly band,
   They move in flesh again.
Once more on Salem's mount they stand
   And show themselves to men.

And so through Him Who conquered Death,
   May we, too, upward press,
From death of sin sweet life to win
   Of truth and holiness;

And like the Saints returning home
   With CHRIST, we pray that we
May to GOD'S Holy City come
   And true Mount Sion see!—Amen.

117

We are but little children weak,
Nor born in any high estate;
What can we do for JESUS' sake,
Who is so high and good and great?

We know the Holy Innocents
Laid down for Him their infant life,
And martyrs brave and patient saints
Have stood for Him in fire and strife.

We wear the cross they wore of old,
Our lips have learned like vows to make;
We need not die, we cannot fight;
What may we do for JESUS' sake?

Oh, day by day, each Christian child
Has much to do, without, within;
A death to die for JESUS' sake,
A weary war to wage with sin.

When deep within our swelling hearts
The thoughts of pride and anger rise,
When bitter words are on our tongues,
And tears of passion in our eyes;

Then we may stay the angry blow,
Then we may check the hasty word,
Give gentle answers back again,
And fight a battle for our LORD.

With smiles of peace, and looks of love,
Light in our dwellings we may make,
Bid kind good-humour brighten there:
And still do all for JESUS' sake.

There's not a child so small and weak
But has his little cross to take;
His little work of love and praise,
That he may do for JESUS' sake.—Amen.

118

For thee, O dear, dear country,
   Mine eyes their vigils keep;
For very love, beholding
   Thy happy name, they weep.
The mention of thy glory
   Is unction to the breast,
And medicine in sickness,
   And love, and life, and rest.

O one, O only mansion!
   O Paradise of joy!
Where tears are ever banished,
   And smiles have no alloy;
The LAMB is all thy splendour;
   The Crucified thy praise;
His laud and benediction
   Thy ransomed people raise.

With jasper glow thy bulwarks,
   Thy streets with emeralds blaze;
The sardius and the topaz
   Unite in thee their rays;
Thine ageless walls are bonded
   With amethyst unpriced;
The Saints build up thy fabric,
   And the corner-stone is CHRIST.

Thou hast no shore, fair ocean!
   Thou hast no time, bright day!
Dear fountain of refreshment
   To pilgrims far away!

Upon the Rock of Ages
  They raise thy holy tower;
Thine is the victor's laurel,
  And thine the golden dower.

O sweet and blessed country,
  The home of GOD's elect!
O sweet and blessed country
  That eager hearts expect!
JESU, in mercy bring us
  To that dear land of rest;
Who art, with GOD the FATHER
  And SPIRIT, ever Blest.—Amen.

119

Jerusalem! my happy home!
  When shall I come to thee?
When shall my sorrows have an end,
  Thy joys when shall I see?

O happy harbour of the Saints,
  O sweet and pleasant soil,
In thee no sorrows may be found,
  No grief, no care, no toil!

Jerusalem! Jerusalem!
  God grant I once may see
Thy endless joys, and of the same
  Partaker aye may be!

Thy walls are made of precious stones,
  Thy bulwarks diamonds square,
Thy gates are of right Orient pearl,
  Exceeding rich and rare.

Thy turrets and thy pinnacles
  With carbuncles do shine;
Thy very streets are paved with gold
  Surpassing clear and fine.

There David stands, with harp in hands,
  As master of the quire;
Ten thousand times that man were blest,
  That might his music hear!

Our Lady sings *Magnificat*
  With tones surpassing sweet,
And all the virgins bear their part,
  Sitting about her feet.

TE DEUM doth Saint Ambrose sing,
  Saint Austin doth the like;
Old Simeon and Zachary
  Have not their songs to seek.

There Magdalene hath left her moan
  And cheerfully doth sing
With blessed saints, whose harmony
  In every street doth ring.

Jerusalem, my happy home,
  Would GOD I were in thee;
Would GOD my woes were at an end,
  Thy joys that I might see!—Amen.

120

Above the clear blue sky,
  In Heaven's bright abode,
The angel host on high
  Sing praises to their GOD.
    Allelulia!
    They love to sing,
    To GOD their King,
    Alleluia!

But GOD from infant tongues,
  On earth receiveth praise,
We then our cheerful songs
  In sweet accord will raise,

Alleluia!
We too will sing
To GOD our King.
Alleluia!

O blessed LORD, Thy truth
  To us Thy babes impart,
And teach us in our youth
  To know Thee as Thou art.
Alleluia!
Then shall we sing
To GOD our King,
Alleluia!

Oh, may Thy holy Word
  Spread all the world around
And all with one accord
  Uplift the joyful sound,
Alleluia!
All then shall sing
To GOD their King,
Alleluia!—Amen.

121

Pleasant are Thy courts above
In the land of light and love;
Pleasant are Thy courts below
In this land of sin and woe.
Oh, my spirit longs and faints
For the converse of Thy Saints,
For the brightness of Thy Face,
For Thy fullness, GOD of grace.

Happy birds that sing and fly
Round Thy altars, O Most High;
Happier souls that find a rest
In a heavenly FATHER's breast;
Like the wandering dove that found

No repose on earth around,
They can to their ark repair,
And enjoy it ever there.

Happy souls, their praises flow
Even in this vale of woe;
Waters in the desert rise,
Manna feeds them from the skies;
On they go from strength to strength,
Till they reach Thy Throne at length,
At Thy Feet adoring fall,
Who hast led them safe through all.

Lord, be mine this prize to win,
Guide me through a world of sin,
Keep me by Thy saving grace,
Give me at Thy Side a place.
Sun and Shield alike Thou art,
Guide and guard my erring heart;
Grace and glory flow from Thee;
Shower, oh, shower them, Lord, on me.
—Amen.

122

Come sing with holy gladness
  High Alleluias sing;
Uplift your loud Hosannas
  To Jesus, Lord and King:
Sing, boys, in joyful chorus
  Your hymn of praise to-day;
And sing, ye gentle maidens,
  Your sweet responsive lay.

'Tis good for boys and maidens
  Sweet hymns to Christ to sing;
'Tis meet that children's voices
  Should praise the children's King:

For JESUS is salvation,
   And glory, grace, and rest;
To babe, and boy, and maiden
   The one Redeemer Blest.

O boys, be strong in JESUS!
   To toil for Him is gain;
And JESUS wrought with Joseph
   With chisel, saw and plane.
O maidens, live for JESUS,
   Who was a maiden's Son!
Be patient, pure, and gentle,
   And perfect grace begun.

Soon in the golden city
   The boys and girls shall play,
And through the dazzling mansions
   Rejoice in endless day.
O CHRIST, prepare Thy children
   With that triumphant throng
To pass the burnished portals,
   And sing the eternal song.—Amen.

123

See amid the winter's snow,
Born for us on earth below;
See the tender Lamb appears,
Promised from eternal years.

        CHORUS.
   Hail, thou ever-blessed morn;
   Hail, redemption's happy dawn!
   Sing through all Jerusalem,
   CHRIST is born in Bethlehem.

Lo, within the manger lies
He Who built the starry skies;
He Who, throned in height sublime,
Sits amid the Cherubim!
   Hail, thou ever-blessed, &c.

Say, ye holy shepherds, say,
What your joyful news to-day;
Wherefore have ye left your sheep
On the lowly mountain steep?
 Hail, thou ever-blessed, &c.

"As we watched at dead of night,
Lo, we saw a wondrous light;
Angels singing peace on earth,
Told us of the Saviour's birth."
 Hail, thou ever-blessed, &c.

Sacred Infant, all divine,
What a tender love was Thine,
Thus to come from highest bliss
Down to such a world as this!
 Hail, thou ever-blessed, &c.

Teach, oh, teach us, Holy Child,
By Thy Face so meek and mild,
Teach us to resemble Thee,
In Thy sweet humility.
 Hail, thou ever-blessed, &c.

124

Brightly gleams our banner,
 Pointing to the sky,
Waving on CHRIST'S soldiers
 To their home on high!
Marching through the desert,
 Gladly thus we pray,
Still with hearts united,
 Singing on our way—

  Brightly gleams our banner,
   Pointing to the sky,
  Waving on CHRIST'S soldiers
   To their home on high!

Jesu, Lord and Master,
  At Thy sacred Feet,
Here, with hearts rejoicing,
  See Thy children meet,
Often have we left Thee,
  Often gone astray;
Keep us, mighty Saviour,
  In the narrow way.
    Brightly gleams, &c.

Pattern of our childhood,
  Once Thyself a Child,
Make our childhood holy,
  Pure, and meek, and mild.
In the hour of danger
  Whither can we flee,
Save to Thee, dear Saviour,
  Only unto Thee?
    Brightly gleams, &c.

All our days direct us
  In the way we go;
Crown us still victorious
  Over every foe:
Bid Thine Angels shield us
  When the storm-clouds lour;
Pardon Thou and save us
  In the last dread hour.
    Brightly gleams, &c.

Then with saints and Angels
  May we join above,
Offering prayers and praises
  At Thy Throne of love.
When the march is over,
  Then come rest and peace,
Jesus in His beauty!
  Songs that never cease!
    Brightly gleams, &c.—Amen.

125

Oft in danger, oft in woe,
Onward, Christians, onward go;
Bear the toil, maintain the strife,
Strengthened with the Bread of Life.

Let not sorrow dim your eye,
Soon shall every tear be dry;
Let not fear your course impede,
Great your strength, if great your need.

Let your drooping hearts be glad;
March in heavenly armour clad:
Fight, nor think the battle long,
Soon shall victory wake your song.

Onward then to glory move;
More than conquerors ye shall prove;
Though opposed by many a foe,
Christian soldiers, onward go!

Hymns of glory and of praise,
FATHER unto Thee we raise,
Holy JESUS, praise to Thee
With the SPIRIT ever be.—Amen.

126

SAVIOUR, blessed Saviour,
  Listen whilst we sing,
Hearts and voices raising
  Praises to our King;
All we have to offer,
  All we hope to be,
Body, soul, and spirit,
  All we yield to Thee.

Nearer, ever nearer,
  CHRIST, we draw to Thee;
Deep in adoration,
  Bending low the knee;

Thou for our redemption
  Cam'st on earth to die;
Thou that we might follow,
  Hast gone up on high.

Onward, ever onward,
  Journeying o'er the road;
Worn by saints before us,
  Journeying on to GOD;
Leaving all behind us,
  May we hasten on,
Backward never looking
  Till the prize is won.

Higher, then, and higher,
  Bear the ransomed soul,
Earthly toils forgotten,
  Saviour, to its goal;
Where, in joys unthought of,
  Saints with Angels sing,
Never weary, raising
  Praises to their King.—Amen.

127

Brightest and best of the sons of the morning
Dawn on our darkness, and lend us thine aid!
Star of the East, the horizon adorning,
Guide where our Infant REDEEMER is laid!

Cold on Thy cradle the dew-drops are shining;
Low lies Thy Head with the beasts of the stall;
Angels adore Thee, in slumber reclining,
Maker and Monarch and SAVIOUR of all.

Say, shall we yield Thee, in costly devotion;
Odours of Edom and offerings Divine!
Gems of the mountain, and pearls of the ocean,
Myrrh from the forest, or gold from the mine?

Yet may we offer more ample oblation;
Love, more than gold, shall Thy favour secure;
Richest of myrrh is the heart's adoration;
Sweetest of incense the prayer of the pure.

Brightest and best of the sons of the morning!
Dawn on our darkness, and lend us thine aid!
Star of the East, the horizon adorning,
Guide where our Infant REDEEMER is laid! —Amen.

128

Oh, what the joy and the glory must be,
Those endless Sabbaths the blessed ones see!
Crown for the valiant, to weary ones rest;
GOD shall be All and in all ever blest.

What are the Monarch, His Court, and His Throne?
What are the peace and the joy that they own?
Oh that the blest ones, who in it have share,
All that they feel could as fully declare!

(116)

Truly Jerusalem name we that shore,
Vision of peace, that brings joy ever-
    more;
Wish and fulfilment can severed be
    ne'er,
Nor the thing prayed for come short of
    the prayer.

There, where no troubles distraction can
    bring,
We the sweet anthems of Sion shall sing;
While for Thy grace, LORD, their voices
    of praise
Thy blessed people eternally raise.

There dawns no Sabbath, no Sabbath is
    o'er,
Those Sabbath-keepers have one ever-
    more;
One and unending is that triumph-song
Which to the Angels and us shall belong.

Now in the meanwhile, with hearts
    raised on high,
We for that country must yearn and must
    sigh;
Seeking Jerusalem, dear native land,
Through our long exile on Babylon's
    strand.

Low before Him with our praises we fall
Of Whom, and in Whom, and through
    Whom are all;
Of Whom, the FATHER; and in Whom,
    the SON;
Through Whom, the SPIRIT, with them
    ever ONE.   —Amen.

129

Hark, the sound of holy voices, chant-
 ing at the crystal sea,
Alleluia! Alleluia! Alleluia! Lord, to
 Thee.
Multitude which none can number, like
 the stars in glory stands,
Clothed in white apparel, holding palms
 of victory in their hands.

Patriarch, and holy Prophet, who pre-
 pared the way of Christ,
King, Apostle, Saint, Confessor, Martyr,
 and Evangelist,
Saintly maiden, godly matron, widows
 who have watched to prayer,
Joined in holy concert, singing to the
 Lord of all, are there.

They have come from tribulation, and
 have washed their robes in Blood,
Washed them in the Blood of Jesus;
 tried they were, and firm they stood;
Mocked, imprisoned, stoned, tormented,
 sawn asunder, slain with sword,
They have conquered Death and Satan
 by the might of Christ the Lord.

Marching with Thy Cross their banner,
 they have triumphed, following
Thee, the Captain of salvation—Thee,
 their Saviour and their King;
Gladly, Lord, with Thee they suffered;
 gladly, Lord, with Thee they died;
And by death to life immortal they were
 born and glorified.

Now they reign in heavenly glory, now
  they walk in golden light,
Now they drink, as from a river, holy
  bliss and infinite;
Love and peace they taste for ever, and
  all truth and knowledge see
In the beatific vision of the Blessed
  TRINITY.

GOD of GOD, the One-begotten LIGHT
  of LIGHT, EMMANUEL,
In Whose Body joined together all the
  saints for ever dwell,
Pour upon us of Thy fulness, that we
  may for evermore
GOD the FATHER, GOD the SON, and
  GOD the HOLY GHOST adore.
  —Amen.

130

Lead us, Heavenly FATHER, lead us
  O'er the world's tempestuous sea;
Guide us, guard us, keep us, feed us,
  For we have no help but Thee,
Yet possessing every blessing,
  If our GOD our FATHER be.

SAVIOUR, breathe forgiveness o'er us,
  All our weakness Thou dost know;
Thou didst tread this earth before us,
  Thou didst feel its keenest woe;
Lone and dreary, faint and weary,
  Through the desert Thou didst go.

SPIRIT of our GOD, descending,
  Fill our hearts with heavenly joy,
Love with every passion blending,
  Pleasure that can never cloy;
Thus provided, pardoned, guided,
  Nothing can our peace destroy.
  —Amen.

131

For all the saints who from their labours rest,
Who Thee by faith before the world confessed,
Thy Name, O JESU, be for ever blest.
 Alleluia!

Thou wast their Rock, their Fortress, and their Might;
Thou, LORD, their Captain in the well-fought fight;
Thou in the darkness drear their one true Light.
 Alleluia!

For the Apostles' glorious company,
Who, bearing forth the cross o'er land and sea,
Shook all the mighty world, we sing to Thee.
 Alleluia!

For the Evangelists, by whose pure word,
Like fourfold streams, the garden of the LORD
Is fair and fruitful, be Thy Name adored.
 Alleluia!

For Martyrs, who with rapture-kindled eye,
Saw the bright crown descending from the sky,
And dying, grasped it, Thee we glorify.
 Alleluia!

Oh, may Thy soldiers, faithful, true, and bold,
Fight as the Saints who nobly fought of old,
And win, with them, the victor's crown of gold.
 Alleluia!

Oh, blest communion! fellowship divine!
We feebly struggle; they in glory shine!
Yet all are one in Thee, for all are Thine.
    Alleluia!

And when the strife is fierce, the warfare long,
Steals on the ear the distant triumph-song,
And hearts are brave again, and arms are strong.   Alleluia!

The golden evening brightens in the west:
Soon, soon, to faithful warriors cometh rest;
Sweet is the calm of Paradise the blest.
    Alleluia!

But lo, there breaks a yet more glorious day!
The saints triumphant rise in bright array!
The King of Glory passes on His way.
    Alleluia!

From earth's wide bounds, from ocean's farthest coast,
Through gates of pearl streams on the countless host,
Singing to FATHER, SON, and HOLY GHOST.   Alleluia!—Amen.

132

Lift up, lift up, ye heavenly gates,
 Lift up your heads on high;
Throw wide the everlasting doors,
 The LORD of HOSTS draws nigh.

With lowly mien a heavenly maid,
   Her GOD upon her breast,
Appears before the temple gates,
   The ever Virgin bless'd;
The saintly Joseph walks beside,
And guards the Babe and Virgin Bride.

The maid of Royal Judah's line,
   The Mother of our King,
Bears to His courts two gentle doves,
   Her humble offering.
And so within the temple gates,
The Holy Family awaits.

Angelic hosts, through gates of pearl,
   Portals all wrought with gold,
With chalcedon and topaz set,
   And gems of wealth untold;
Look down upon the holy sight,
And chant, with anthems of delight.

O bless'd is she who, born of Eve,
   Hath borne the Eternal Son,
We hail her with an Ave sweet,
   Who this high grace hath won.
But bless'd with her, who enter in
That City's gates, all cleansed from sin.

Then praise we Him, Who sits in power
   Upon the sapphire Throne,
And praise we Him, Sweet Mary's SON,
   And HOLY SPIRIT—ONE.
May we be of that Blessed Throng,
Who praise Thee in the Victor's song.

Lift up, lift up, ye heavenly gates,
   Lift up your heads on high;
Thrown wide henceforth th' eternal doors,
   Bright portals of the sky.   —AMEN.

133

Alleluia, song of sweetness.
  Voice of joy that cannot die;
Alleluia is the anthem
  Ever dear to choirs on high;
In the House of GOD abiding
  Thus they sing eternally.

Alleluia thou resoundest,
  True Jerusalem and free;
Alleluia, joyful Mother.
  All thy children sing with thee;
But by Babylon's sad waters
  Mourning exiles now are we.

Alleluia cannot always
  Be our song while here below;
Alleluia our transgressions
  Make us for awhile forego;
For the solemn time is coming
  When our tears for sin must flow.

Therefore in our hymns we pray Thee,
  Grant us, Blessed TRINITY.
At the last to keep Thine Easter
  In our Home beyond the sky,
There to Thee for ever singing
  Alleluia joyfully.—Amen.

134

The SON of GOD goes forth to war,
  A kingly crown to gain.
His blood-red banner streams afar;
  Who follows in His train?
Who best can drink his cup of woe,
  Triumphant over pain,
Who patient bears his cross below,
  He follows in His train.

The martyr first, whose eagle eye
   Could pierce beyond the grave,
Who saw his Master in the sky,
   And called on Him to save.
Like Him, with pardon on his tongue,
   In midst of mortal pain,
He prayed for them that did the wrong;
   Who follows in His train?

A glorious band, the chosen few
   On whom the SPIRIT came.
Twelve valiant saints, their hope they knew,
   And mocked the cross and flame.
They met the tyrant's brandished steel,
   The lion's gory mane,
They bowed their necks, the death to feel;
   Who follows in their train?

A noble army, men and boys,
   The matron and the maid,
Around the SAVIOUR'S Throne rejoice,
   In robes of light arrayed.
They climbed the steep ascent of Heaven
   Through peril, toil, and pain;
O GOD, to us may grace be given
   To follow in their train.—Amen.

135

Jesu meek and gentle,
   SON of GOD most high;
Pitying, loving SAVIOUR,
   Hear Thy children's cry.

Pardon our offences.
   Loose our captive chains,
Break down every idol,
   Which our soul detains.

Give us holy freedom.
  Fill our hearts with love;
Draw us, Holy JESU!
  To the realms above.

Lead us on our journey,
  Be Thyself the Way,
Through terrestrial darkness,
  To celestial day.

JESU! meek and gentle,
  SON of GOD most high!
Pitying, loving SAVIOUR,
  Hear Thy Children's cry.—Amen.

136

Great GOD, what do I see and hear?
  The end of things created:
The Judge of all men doth appear
  On clouds of glory seated;
The trumpet sounds, the graves restore
The dead which they contained before;
  Prepare my soul, to meet Him.

The dead in CHRIST are first to rise
  At that last trumpet's sounding;
Caught up to meet Him in the skies,
  With joy their LORD surrounding;
No gloomy fears their souls dismay;
His presence sheds eternal day
  On those prepared to meet Him.

The ungodly, filled with guilty fears,
  Behold His wrath prevailing;
In woe they rise, but all their tears
  And sighs are unavailing;
The day of grace is past and gone;
Trembling they stand before His Throne,
  All unprepared to meet Him.

Great Judge, to Thee our prayers we
    pour,
  In deep abasement bending;
O shield us through that last dread hour,
  Thy wondrous love extending;
May we, in this our trial day,
With faithful hearts Thy Word obey,
  And thus prepare to meet Thee.
—Amen.

137

The Saints all crowned with glory,
  In Heaven's eternal day,
To JESUS, our Redeemer,
  For our salvation pray.
    The Saints, our dearest brothers,
      Who now with JESUS dwell;
    The world may scorn and mock them,
      But we will love them well.

We love that Sacred Virgin,
  The Mother of our God;
We love the LORD's Apostles,
  Who in His footsteps trod.
    The Saints, &c.

We love the noble Martyrs,
  The Virgin choir we love;
The Matrons and Confessors,
  And all the Saints above.
    The Saints, &c.

Then JESU, let Thy Mother
  And all the Saints entreat
That we may share Thy glory,
  And worship at Thy feet.
    The Saints, &c.

138

Lord of our life, and God of our salvation,
Star of our night, and Hope of every nation,
Hear and receive Thy Church's supplication,
    Lord God Almighty.

See round Thine ark the hungry billows curling;
See how Thy foes their banners are unfurling;
Lord, while their darts envenomed they are hurling.
    Thou canst preserve us.

Lord, Thou canst help when earthly armour faileth,
Lord, Thou canst save when deadly sin assaileth,
Lord, o'er Thy Church nor death nor hell prevaileth:
    Grant us Thy peace, Lord.

Grant us Thy help till foes are backward driven,
Grant them Thy truth, that they may be forgiven,
Grant peace on earth, and, after we have striven,
    Peace in Thy heaven.—Amen.

139

Children of the Heavenly King,
As ye journey sweetly sing;
Sing your Saviour's worthy praise,
Glorious in His works and ways.

We are travelling home to GOD,
In the way the fathers trod;
They are happy now, and we
Soon their happiness shall see.

Fear not, brethren, joyful stand
On the borders of your land;
JESUS CHRIST, the FATHER'S SON,
Bids you undismayed go on.

LORD, obediently we go,
Gladly leaving all below;
Only Thou our Leader be,
And we still will follow Thee.

Hymns of glory and of praise,
FATHER, unto Thee we raise;
Praise to Thee, O CHRIST, our King,
And the HOLY GHOST, we sing.
—Amen.

140

The Saints of GOD! Their conflict past,
And life's long battle won at last,
No more they need the shield or sword,
They cast them down before their LORD:
  O happy Saints! forever blest,
  At JESUS' feet how safe your rest!

The Saints of GOD! Their wandering done,
No more their weary course they run,
No more they faint, no more they fall,
No foes oppress, no fears appal:—
  O happy Saints! forever blest,
  In that dear home how sweet your rest!

The Saints of GOD! Life's voyage o'er,
Safe landed on that blissful shore,
No stormy tempests now they dread,
No roaring billows lift their head:—

O happy Saints! forever blest,
In that calm haven of your rest!

The Saints of GOD their vigil keep
While yet their mortal bodies sleep,
Till from the dust they too shall rise
And soar triumphant to the skies:—
O happy Saints! rejoice and sing,
He quickly comes, your LORD and King

O GOD of Saints! to Thee we cry;
O SAVIOUR! plead for us on high;
O HOLY GHOST! our Guide and Friend,
Grant us Thy grace till life shall end;
That with All Saints our rest may be!
In that bright Paradise with Thee!
—Amen.

141

The first Nowell the Angel did say
Was to certain poor shepherds in fields
    as they lay—
In fields where they lay keeping their
    sheep,
On a cold winter's night that was so deep.

CHO.—Nowell, Nowell, Nowell, Nowell,
    Born is the King of Israel.

They looked up and saw a star
Shining in the East, beyond them far,
And to the earth it gave great light,
And so it continued both day and night.
    Nowell. &c.

And by the light of that same star
Three wise men came from country far;
To seek for a King, was their intent,
And to follow the star wherever it went.
    Nowell. &c.

This star drew nigh to the north-west,
O'er Bethlehem it took its rest;
And there it did both stop and stay,
Right over the place where JESUS lay.
    Nowell, &c.

Then entered in those wise men three.
Full reverently upon their knee,
And offered there in His presence
Their gold and myrrh, and frankincense.
    Nowell, &c.

Then let us all with one accord
Sing praises to our Heavenly LORD;
That hath made Heaven and earth of nought,
And with His Blood mankind hath bought.
    Nowell, &c.—Amen.

142

On Jordan's bank the Baptist's cry
Announces that the LORD is nigh;
Awake, and harken, for he brings
Glad tidings of the King of kings.

Then cleansed be every breast from sin;
Make straight the way for GOD within;
Prepare we in our hearts a home,
Where such a mighty Guest may come.

For Thou art our Salvation, LORD,
Our Refuge, and our great Reward;
Without Thy grace we waste away,
Like flowers that wither and decay.

To heal the sick stretch out Thine Hand,
And bid the fallen sinner stand;
Shine forth, and let Thy light restore
Earth's own true loveliness once more.

All praise, Eternal SON, to Thee
Whose Advent doth Thy people free,
Whom with the FATHER we adore
And HOLY GHOST for evermore.—Amen.

143

Have mercy on us, GOD most High,
  Who lift our hearts to Thee;
Have mercy on us worms of earth,
  Most Holy TRINITY.

Most ancient of all mysteries!
  Before Thy Throne we lie;
Have mercy now, most Merciful,
  Most Holy TRINITY.

When heaven and earth were yet unmade,
  When time was yet unknown,
Thou, in Thy bliss and majesty,
  Didst live and love alone.

How wonderful creation is,
  The work that Thou didst bless;
And oh, what then must Thou be like,
  Eternal Loveliness!

Most ancient of all mysteries!
  Low at Thy Throne we lie;
Have mercy now, most Merciful,
  Most Holy TRINITY.—Amen.

144

Now my tongue, the mystery telling,
  Of the glorious Body sing,
And the Blood, all price excelling,
  Which the Gentiles' LORD and King,
In a Virgin's womb once dwelling,
  Shed for this world's ransoming.

Given for us, and condescending
    To be born for us below,
He, with men in converse blending,
    Dwelt the seed of truth to sow,
Till he closed with wondrous ending
    His most patient life of woe.

That last night, at supper lying,
    'Mid the Twelve, His chosen band,
Jesus, with the law complying,
    Keeps the feasts its rites demand;
Then, more precious Food supplying,
    Gives Himself with His own Hand.

Word-made-Flesh true bread He maketh
    By His Word His Flesh to be;
Wine His Blood; which whoso taketh
    Must from carnal thoughts be free;
Faith alone, though sight forsaketh,
    Shews true hearts the mystery.—Amen.

145

O come, O come, Emmanuel,
And ransom captive Israel,
That mourns in lonely exile here,
Until the Son of God appear.
    Rejoice! Rejoice! Emmanuel
    Shall come to thee, O Israel.

O come, Thou Rod of Jesse, free
Thine own from Satan's tyranny;
From depths of hell Thy people save,
And give them victory o'er the grave.
    Rejoice! Rejoice! Emmanuel
    Shall come to thee, O Israel.

O come, Thou Day-spring, come and cheer
Our spirits by Thine Advent here:
Disperse the gloomy clouds of night,
And death's dark shadows put to flight.
    Rejoice! Rejoice! Emmanuel
    Shall come to thee, O Israel.

O come, Thou Key of David, come,
And open wide our heavenly home;
Make safe the way that leads on high,
And close the path to misery.
    Rejoice! Rejoice! Emmanuel
    Shall come to thee, O Israel.

O come, O come, Thou LORD of Might,
Who to Thy tribes, on Sinai's height,
In ancient times didst give the law
In cloud, and majesty, and awe.
    Rejoice! Rejoice! Emmanuel
    Shall come to thee, O Israel.—Amen.

146

Sun of my soul, Thou SAVIOUR dear,
It is not night if Thou be near;
O may no earth-born cloud arise
To hide Thee from Thy servant's eyes.

When the soft dews of kindly sleep
My wearied eyelids gently steep,
Be my last thought how sweet to rest
Forever on my SAVIOUR's breast.

Abide with me from morn till eve,
For without Thee I cannot live;
Abide with me when night is nigh,
For without Thee I dare not die.

If some poor wandering child of Thine
Have spurned to-day the voice divine,
Now, LORD, the gracious work begin;
Let him no more lie down in sin.

Watch by the sick; enrich the poor
With blessings from Thy boundless store:
Be every mourner's sleep to-night,
Like infant's slumbers, pure and light.

Come near and bless us when we wake,
Ere through the world our way we take,
Till in the ocean of Thy love
We lose ourselves in Heaven above.
—Amen.

147

Brother, now thy toils are o'er;
   Fought the battle, won the crown;
On life's rough and barren shore
   Thou hast laid thy burden down:
Grant *him,* LORD, Eternal Rest
With the Spirits of the Blest.

Through death's valley dim and dark
   JESUS guide thee in the gloom,
Shew thee where His footprints mark
   Tracks of glory through the Tomb:
Grant *him,* LORD, Eternal Rest
With the Spirits of the Blest.

Angels bear thee to the land
   Where the towers of Sion rise,
Safely lead thee by the hand
   To the fields of Paradise:
Grant *him,* LORD, Eternal Rest
With the Spirits of the Blest.

White-robed at the golden Gate
   Of the New Jerusalem
May the Host of Martyrs wait,—
   Give thee part and lot with them.
Grant *him*, LORD, Eternal Rest
With the Spirits of the Blest.

Friends and dear ones, gone before
   To the land of endless peace,
Meet thee on that further shore
   Where all tears and sorrows cease.
Grant *him*, LORD, Eternal Rest
With the Spirits of the Blest.

There the LORD of Life and Love
   Wipes the tear from every eye;
To the courts of bliss above
   Pain and suffering come not nigh:
Grant *him*, LORD, Eternal Rest
With the Spirits of the Blest.

Sun by day nor moon by night
   Cast their beams about the Throne,
For the Lamb sheds there His Light
   On the foreheads of His Own:
Grant *him*, LORD, Eternal Rest
With the Spirits of the Blest.

Earth to earth, and dust to dust,
   Clay we give to kindred clay,
In the sure and certain trust
   Of the Resurrection Day:
Grant *him*, LORD, Eternal Rest
With the Spirits of the Blest.

CHRIST the Sower sows thee here:
   When the Eternal Day shall dawn
He will gather in the ear
   On that Resurrection Morn:
Grant *him*, LORD, Eternal Rest
With the Spirits of the Blest.—Amen.

148

Abide with me; fast falls the eventide;
The darkness deepens; LORD, with me abide;
When other helpers fail, and comforts flee,
Help of the helpless, O abide with me.

Swift to its close ebbs out life's little day;
Earth's joys grow dim, its glories pass away;
Change and decay in all around I see;
O Thou Who changest not, abide with me.

I need Thy presence every passing hour;
What but Thy grace can foil the tempter's power?
Who like Thyself my guide and stay can be?
Through cloud and sunshine, LORD, abide with me.

I fear no foe with Thee at hand to bless;
Ills have no weight, and tears no bitterness;
Where is death's sting? Where, grave, thy victory?
I triumph still, if Thou abide with me.

Hold Thou Thy Cross before my closing eyes,
Shine through the gloom, and point me to the skies;
Heaven's morning breaks, and earth's vain shadows flee;
In life, in death, O LORD, abide with me.
—Amen.

149

Jesu we adore Thee,
   Veiled 'neath bread and wine,
Though not yet Thy glory
   On our sight may shine.
What Thy word commanded
   Duly is fulfilled,
And Thyself art present,
   As Thyself hast willed.

As in Bethlehem's manger,
   As on Calvary's hill,
Faithful hearts adored Thee,
   We adore Thee still.
When the Bread is broken,
   And the Wine outpoured,
We, with the Apostles,
   Cry "It is the LORD!"

Lamb of God, Who takest
   All our sin away,
Cleanse our hearts and fill us
   With Thy love, we pray.
Once a sinless Victim,
   Thou for sin didst bleed;
Now, our Priest for ever,
   Thou wilt intercede.

Saints their crowns of glory
   Cast before Thy Feet,
Throngs of holy Angels
   Offer incense sweet,
Yet our feeble praises
   Thou wilt not despise,
Heavenward they are rising,
   With Thy Sacrifice.
                —Amen.

150

Jerusalem the golden,
  With milk and honey blest,
Beneath thy contemplation
  Sink heart and voice opprest.
I know not, oh, I know not
  What joys await us there,
What radiancy of glory,
  What bliss beyond compare.

They stand, those halls of Sion,
  All jubilant with song,
And bright with many an Angel,
  And all the martyr throng;
The Prince is ever in them,
  The daylight is serene;
The pastures of the blessed
  Are decked in glorious sheen.

There is the throne of David;
  And there, from care released,
The shout of them that triumph,
  The song of them that feast;
And they, who with their Leader
  Have conquered in the fight,
For ever and for ever
  Are clad in robes of white.

Oh, sweet and blessed country,
  The home of GOD's elect!
Oh, sweet and blessed country,
  That eager hearts expect!
JESU, in mercy bring us
  To that dear land of rest;
Who art, with GOD the FATHER
  And SPIRIT, ever Blest.
              —Amen.

151

There is one True and only God,
  Our Maker and our Lord;
And He created everything
  By His Almighty Word.
    All this, and all the Church doth teach,
      My God! I do believe!
    For Thou hast bid us hear the Church,
      And Thou canst not deceive.

But in this One and Only God
  There yet are Persons Three:
The Father, Son, and Holy Ghost,
  One Blessed Trinity.—All this, &c.

The Second Person, God the Son,
  Came down on earth to dwell;
Took Flesh, and died upon the Cross,
  To save from sin and hell.—All this, &c.

The Holy Spirit I adore,
  The Source of life and love,
Who through the veins of Holy Church
  As sap in plants doth move.
    —All this &c.

The good with God in Heaven above
  Will ever happy be;
The wicked in the flames of hell
  Will burn eternally.—All this, &c.
        —Amen.

152

Holy, Holy, Holy! Lord God Almighty!
  Early in the morning our song shall rise
    to Thee;
Holy, Holy, Holy! merciful and mighty!
  God in Three Persons, Blessed
    Trinity!

Holy, Holy, Holy! all the saints adore Thee,
  Casting down their golden crowns around the glassy sea;
Cherubim and Seraphim falling down before Thee,
  Which wert, and art, and evermore shalt be.

Holy, Holy, Holy! though the darkness hide Thee,
  Though the eye of sinful man Thy glory may not see,
Only Thou art holy; there is none beside Thee
  Perfect in power, in love, and purity.

Holy, Holy, Holy! LORD GOD Almighty!
  All Thy works shall praise Thy Name, in earth, and sky, and sea;
Holy, Holy, Holy! Merciful and Mighty!
  GOD in THREE PERSONS, Blessed TRINITY.—Amen.

153

O come, all ye faithful,
Joyful and triumphant,
O come ye, O come ye, to Bethlehem;
Come and behold Him
Born, the King of Angels;
O come, let us adore Him,
O come, let us adore Him,
O come, let us adore Him, CHRIST the LORD.

GOD of GOD,
LIGHT of LIGHT,
Lo! He abhors not the Virgin's womb;

  Very GOD,
   Begotten, not created;
 O come, let us adore Him, &c.

   Sing, choirs of angels,
   Sing in exultation,
 Sing, all ye citizens of heaven above,
   Glory to GOD
   In the highest;
 O come, let us adore Him, &c.

   Yea, LORD, we greet Thee,
   Born this happy morning;
 JESU, to Thee be glory given;
   WORD of the FATHER,
   Now in flesh appearing,
   O come, let us adore Him,
 O come, let us adore Him, CHRIST the
   LORD.—Amen.

154

 JESU, in loving worship
  Thy little children fall,
Thy tender lambs hear gladly
  Their loving Shepherd's call.
May Arms, which once so fondly
  Took infants to Thy Breast,
Enfold us, as Thou callest—
  "Come unto Me and rest."

We cannot see Thy glory;
  Not yet our feeble sight
Could bear to gaze upon Thee
  Arrayed in dazzling Light;
But sweet it is to worship
  Thy Blessed Presence here,
And tell Thee how we love Thee,
  As drawest Thou so near.

We plead what now Thou showest
    Before the Father's Throne—
That we may be forgiven
    The wrong that we have done:
We plead Thy Crucifixion
    And pray that never more
By sin we may offend Thee,
    But, penitent, adore.

Each blessed Sunday morning
    We see Thy Blood outpoured,
We see Thy Body broken,
    Thou mercy-loving LORD!
With Angels and Archangels,
    We three times "Holy" sing,
Hosanna in the Highest,
    Hosanna to our King!—Amen.

155

CHRIST, Who once amongst us
    As a Child did dwell,
Is the children's SAVIOUR,
    And He loves us well;
We must keep our promise
    Made Him at the font,
Since He is our Shepherd,
    That we may not want.

There it was they laid us
    In those tender Arms,
Where the lambs are carried
    Safe from all alarms;
If we trust His promise,
    He will let us rest
In His Arms for ever,
    Leaning on His Breast.

Though we may not see Him
    For a little while,
We shall know He holds us,
    Often feel His smile;

Death will be to slumber
  In that sweet embrace,
And we shall awaken
  To behold His Face.

He will be our Shepherd
  After as before,
By still heavenly waters
  Lead us evermore,
Make us lie in pastures
  Beautiful and green,
Where none thirst or hunger,
  And no tears are seen.

Jesus, our good Shepherd,
  Laying down Thy Life,
Lest Thy sheep should perish
  In the cruel strife;
Help us to remember
  All Thy love and care,
Trust in Thee, and love Thee
  Always, everywhere.—Amen.

156

Jesu, gentlest Saviour,
  God of Might and Power,
Thou Thyself art dwelling
  In us at this hour.

Out beyond the shining
  Of the farthest star,
Thou art ever stretching
  Infinitely far.

Yet the hearts of children
  Hold what worlds cannot,
And the God of Wonders
  Loves the lowly spot.

Multiply our Graces,
   Chiefly Love and Fear,
And, dear LORD, the chiefest,
   Grace to persevere.

Oh, how can we thank Thee
   For a Gift like this,
Gift that truly maketh
   Heaven's eternal bliss!

Oh, when wilt Thou always
   Make our hearts Thy home;
We must wait for heaven,
   Then the day will come.——Amen.

157

Hark, my soul! it is the LORD;
'Tis thy SAVIOUR, hear His Word;
JESUS speaks, and speaks to thee,
"Say, poor sinner, lov'st thou Me?

"I delivered thee when bound,
And, when bleeding, healed thy wound;
Sought thee wandering, set thee right,
Turned thy darkness into light.

"Can a woman's tender care
Cease towards the child she bare?
Yes, she may forgetful be,
Yet will I remember thee.

'Mine is an unchanging love,
Higher than the heights above,
Deeper than the depths beneath,
Free and faithful, strong as death.

'Thou shalt see My glory soon,
When the work of grace is done;
Partner of My Throne shall be;
Say, poor sinner, lov'st thou Me?"

Lord, it is my chief complaint
That my love is weak and faint;
Yet I love Thee, and adore:
Oh, for grace to love Thee more.—Amen.

158

How sweet the Name of Jesus sounds
  In a believer's ear!
It soothes his sorrows, heals his wounds,
  And drives away his fear.

It makes the wounded spirit whole,
  And calms the troubled breast;
'Tis manna to the hungry soul,
  And to the weary rest.

Dear Name! the rock on which I build,
  My shield and hiding-place,
My never-failing treasury, filled
  With boundless stores of grace.

Jesus! my Shepherd, Brother, Friend,
  My Prophet, Priest, and King,
My Lord, my Life, my Way, my End,
  Accept the praise I bring.—Amen.

159

From the eastern mountains,
  Pressing on they come,
Wise men in their wisdom,
  To His humble home;
Stirred by deep devotion,
  Hasting from afar,
Ever journeying onward,
  Guided by a star.

There their Lord and Saviour
  Meek and lowly lay,
Wondrous light that led them
  Onward on their way;

Ever now to lighten
  Nations from afar,
As they journey homeward
  By that guiding star.

Thou Who in a manger
  Once hast lowly lain,
Who dost now in glory
  O'er all kingdoms reign,
Gather in the heathen,
  Who in lands afar
Ne'er have seen the brightness
  Of Thy guiding star.

Gather in the outcasts,
  All who go astray,
Throw Thy radiance o'er them,
  Guide them on their way;
Those who never knew Thee,
  Those who wander far,
Guide them by the brightness
  Of Thy guiding star.

Onward through the darkness
  Of the lonely night,
Shining still before them,
  With Thy kindly light,
Guide them, Jew and Gentile,
  Homeward from afar,
Young and old together,
  By Thy kindly star.

Until every nation,
  Whether bond or free,
'Neath Thy starlit banner,
  JESU, follows Thee
O'er the distant mountains,
  To that heavenly home,
Where nor sin nor sorrow
  Evermore shall come.—Amen.

160

O happy band of pilgrims,
   If onward ye will tread,
With JESUS as your Fellow,
   To JESUS as your Head!

O happy if ye labour
   As JESUS did for men!
O happy if ye hunger
   As JESUS hungered then!

The Cross that JESUS carried,
   He carried as your due;
The Crown that JESUS weareth,
   He weareth it for you.

The faith by which ye see Him,
   The hope in which ye yearn,
The love that through all troubles
   To Him alone will turn;

The trials that beset you,
   The sorrows ye endure,
The manifold temptations
   That death alone can cure;

What are they but His jewels,
   Of right celestial worth?
What are they but the ladder
   Set up to heaven on earth?

O happy band of pilgrims,
   Look upward to the skies,
Where such a light affliction
   Shall win so great a prize.—Amen.

161

From Greenland's icy mountains,
   From India's coral strand,
Where Afric's sunny fountains
   Roll down their golden sand;

From many an ancient river,
   From many a palmy plain,
They call as to deliver
   Their land from error's chain.

What though the spicy breezes
   Blow soft o'er Ceylon's isle,
Though every prospect pleases,
   And only man is vile;
In vain with lavish kindness,
   The gifts of GOD are strewn;
The heathen in his blindness,
   Bows down to wood and stone.

Can we, whose souls are lighted
   With wisdom from on high,
Can we, to men benighted,
   The lamp of life deny?
Salvation, oh, salvation!
   The joyful sound proclaim,
Till each remotest nation
   Has learned MESSIAH's Name.

Waft, waft, ye winds, His story,
   And you, ye waters, roll,
Till, like a sea of glory,
   It spreads from pole to pole;
Till o'er our ransomed nature
   The Lamb, for sinners slain,
Redeemer, King, Creator,
   In bliss returns to reign.—Amen.

162

JESU, my LORD, my GOD, my All,
Hear me, blest SAVIOUR, when I call;
Hear me, and from Thy dwelling-place
Pour down the riches of Thy grace:
   JESU, my LORD, I Thee adore,
   Oh, make me love Thee more and more.

Jesu, too late I Thee have sought,
How can I love Thee as I ought?
And how extol Thy matchless fame,
The glorious beauty of Thy Name?
    Jesu, my Lord, &c.

Jesu, what didst Thou find in me,
That Thou hast dealt so lovingly?
How great the joy that Thou hast brought,
So far exceeding hope or thought!
    Jesu, my Lord, &c.

Jesu, of Thee shall be my song,
To Thee my heart and soul belong;
All that I have or am is Thine,
And Thou, blest Saviour, Thou art mine:—Jesu, my Lord, &c.—Amen.

163

Hark! hark, my soul! Angelic songs are swelling
  O'er earth's green fields and ocean's wave-beat shore;
How sweet the truth those blessed strains are telling,
  Of that new life when sin shall be no more!
Angels of Jesus, Angels of light,
Singing to welcome the pilgrims of the night!

Onward we go, for still we hear them singing,
  "Come, weary souls, for Jesus bids you come;"
And through the dark, its echoes sweetly ringing,
  The music of the Gospel leads us home.
Angels of Jesus, Angels of light, &c.

Far, far away, like bells at evening pealing,
  The voice of JESUS sounds o'er land
       and sea,
And laden souls by thousands meekly
       stealing,
  Kind Shepherd, turn their weary steps
      to Thee.
Angels of JESUS, Angels of light, &c.

Rest comes at length; though life be long
      and dreary,
  The day must dawn, and darksome
      night be past;
Faith's journey ends in welcome to the
      weary,
  And Heaven, the heart's true home,
      will come at last;
Angels of JESUS, Angels of light, &c.

Angels! sing on, your faithful watches
      keeping,
  Sing us sweet fragments of the songs
      above;
Till morning's joy shall end the night of
      weeping,
  And life's long shadows break in cloud-
      less love.
Angels of JESUS, Angels of light, &c.
                  —Amen.

164

All hail the power of JESUS' Name;
  Let Angels prostrate fall;
Bring forth the royal diadem
  To crown Him LORD of all.
Crown Him, ye morning stars of light,
  Who fixed this floating ball;
Now hail the Strength of Israel's might,
  And crown Him LORD of all.

Crown Him, ye Martyrs of your GOD,
　Who from His Altar call;
Praise Him whose Blood-stained path ye
　　　trod,
　And crown Him LORD of all.

Ye seed of Israel's chosen race.
　Ye ransomed of the fall,
Hail Him Who saves you by His grace,
　And crown Him LORD of All.

Hail Him, ye heirs of David's line,
　Whom David LORD did call,
The GOD Incarnate, Man Divine,
　And crown Him LORD of all.

Sinners, whose love can ne'er forget
　The wormwood and the gall,
Go spread your trophies at His Feet,
　And crown Him LORD of all.

Let every kindred, every tribe,
　On this terrestrial ball,
To Him all majesty ascribe,
　And crown Him LORD of all.—Amen.

165

Hark! the herald-angels sing
Glory to the new-born KING,
Peace on earth and mercy mild.
GOD and sinners reconciled.
Joyful, all ye nations, rise,
Join the triumph of the skies;
With the angelic host proclaim
CHRIST is born in Bethlehem.
　Hark! the herald-angels sing
　Glory to the new-born KING.

CHRIST, by highest heaven adored,
CHRIST, the Everlasting LORD,
Late in time behold Him come,
Offspring of a Virgin's womb.
Veiled in flesh the GODHEAD see!
Hail, the Incarnate Deity!
Pleased as Man with man to dwell,
JESUS, our EMMANUEL.
   Hark! the herald-angels sing
    Glory to the new-born KING.

Hail, the heaven-born Prince of Peace!
Hail, the Sun of Righteousness!
Light and Life to all He brings,
Risen with healing in His wings.
Mild He lays His glory by,
Born that man no more may die,
Born to raise the sons of earth,
Born to give them second birth.
   Hark! the herald-angels sing
    Glory to the new-born KING.—Amen.

166

Oh grant to each before Thee now
  A meek and lowly heart,
That, like another Mary, we
  May choose the better part,
And at Thy Feet may sit and learn
  To do Thy holy Will,
That thus with highest motive we
  May lowly tasks fulfil.

Let all who hear our tones of love
  Our holy conduct see;
Take knowledge of us, dearest LORD,
  That we have been with Thee.
From all temptations and all sin
  Defend us we implore,
And with Thy Love encompass us
  Both now and evermore.

Oh clothe us with the spotless robe
    That Thy beloved wear,
And in Thy presence let us stand
    Like lilies white and fair;
By earth's defilements all unsoiled,
    A stainless virgin band,
That in Thine Eden we may bloom
    Transplanted by Thy Hand.—Amen.

167

My God, how wonderful Thou art,
    Thy majesty how bright,
How beautiful Thy mercy-seat,
    In depths of burning light!

How dread are Thine eternal years,
    O everlasting Lord,
By prostrate spirits day and night
    Incessantly adored!

How wonderful, how beautiful,
    The sight of Thee must be,
Thine endless wisdom, boundless power
    And awful purity!

Oh, how I fear Thee, living God,
    With deepest, tenderest fears,
And worship Thee with trembling hope,
    And penitential tears!

Yet I may love Thee too, O Lord,
    Almighty as Thou art,
For Thou hast stooped to ask of me
    The love of my poor heart.

No earthly father loves like Thee,
    No mother, e'er so mild,
Bears and forbears as Thou hast done
    With me, Thy sinful child.

Father of Jesus, love's reward,
   What rapture will it be,
Prostrate before Thy Throne to lie,
   And gaze and gaze on Thee.—Amen.

168

Let us now go to Bethlehem,
   To see this wondrous thing,
Mary and Joseph, and with them
   The Babe our Infant King!
Bright Stars above shine on
   To light our speedy way,
While Angels sweetly carol in
   The Blessed Christmas Day.

Let us now go to Bethlehem,
   To see this wondrous thing,
Mary and Joseph, and with them
   The Babe our Infant King!
For we shall find on earth
   The Heaven of Heavens in Him,
The Holy, Holy, Holy Son,
   Beneath the Cherubim.

Let us now go to Bethlehem,
   To see this wondrous thing,
Mary and Joseph, and with them
   The Babe our Infant King!
His Father's Glory come
   To lift our hearts above;
First loved by Him and Angel Hosts,
   We carol back His Love.

Let us now go to Bethlehem,
   Faith's Star shall guide the way
To Jesus cradled in His Church
   This bright Appearing Day!

There, Light's true Light, to Thee
   We sing with glad accord,
For meet it is to celebrate
   Thy Birthday, Jesus Lord!
               —Amen.

169

As with gladness men of old
Did the guiding star behold;
As with joy they hailed its light,
Leading onward, beaming bright;
So, most gracious Lord, may we
Evermore be led to Thee.

As with joyful steps they sped
To that lowly manger bed;
There to bend the knee before
Him Whom heaven and earth adore
So may we with willing feet
Ever seek the mercy-seat.

As they offered gifts most rare
At that manger rude and bare;
So may we with holy joy,
Pure and free from sin's alloy,
All our costliest treasures bring,
Christ! to Thee our heavenly King.

Holy Jesus, every day
Keep us in the narrow way,
And, when earthly things are past,
Bring our ransomed souls at last
Where they need no star to guide,
Where no clouds Thy glory hide.

In the heavenly country bright
Need they no created light;
Thou its Light, its Joy, its Crown,
Thou its Sun which goes not down;
There for ever may we sing
Alleluias to our King.—Amen.

170

I worship Thee, LORD JESU,
  As children did of old,
Who sang within Thy temple,
  Hosannas manifold.

I worship Thee, LORD JESU,
  Who, on Thy Altar laid,
In this most awful Service,
  Our Food and Drink art made.

I worship Thee, LORD JESU,
  Who, in Thy Love divine,
Art hiding here Thy Godhead
  In Forms of Bread and Wine.

I worship Thee, LORD JESU,
  And kneeling unto Thee,
As Thou didst come to Mary,
  I pray Thee, come to me.

I worship Thee, LORD JESU,
  My King and SAVIOUR mild,
Thou hast blest other children,
  Bless also me, Thy child.—Amen.

171

SAVIOUR, again to Thy dear Name we raise
With one accord our parting hymn of praise;
We stand to bless Thee ere our worship cease,
Then, lowly kneeling, wait Thy word of peace.

Grant us Thy peace upon our homeward way;
With Thee began, with Thee shall end the day:
Guard Thou the lips from sin, the hearts from shame
That in this house have called upon Thy Name.

Grant us Thy peace, LORD, thro' the coming night,
Turn Thou for us its darkness into light;
From harm and danger keep Thy children free,
For dark and light are both alike to Thee.

Grant us Thy peace throughout our earthly life,
Our balm in sorrow, and our stay in strife;
Then, when Thy voice shall bid our conflict cease,
Call us, O LORD, to Thine eternal peace.
—Amen.

172

From pain to pain and woe to woe,
  With loving hearts and footsteps slow,
To Calvary with CHRIST we go;
  See how His precious Blood
At every station pours!
  Was ever grief like His?
Was ever sin like ours?

173

Greet the Cross with veneration—
Great its wondrous destination—
  Earth's dread Ransom to sustain;
When we sign this Symbol o'er us,
We the wicked drive before us,
  And from sin a Refuge gain.

From the Tree when Adam taketh
That forbidden fruit, he maketh
  Store of woe for all his heirs;
God the Lord this Tree is bearing,
He the sinner's lot is sharing—
  Sinless, He our loss repairs.

Conquering Tree, with praise we meet thee!
As the world's true Health we greet thee!
  Tribute bring of praise and love.
Thou, the monarch's royal banner,
Be our stair, in mystic manner
  Lead us to the Courts above.

Christ, Thy Cross who sanctifiest,
Death o'ercoming when Thou diest,
  King of earth and Heaven above,
By Thy Passion hear our crying;
And when ends this life of sighing
  Grant us endless joy and love.—Amen.

174

  Lord, in this Thy mercy's day,
  Ere it pass for aye away,
  On our knees we fall and pray.

  Holy Jesu, grant us tears,
  Fill us with heart-searching fears,
  Ere that awful doom appears.

Lord, on us Thy Spirit pour,
Kneeling lowly at the door,
Ere it close for evermore.

By Thy night of agony,
By Thy supplicating cry,
By Thy willingness to die,

By Thy tears of bitter woe
For Jerusalem below,
Let us not Thy love forego.

Grant us 'neath Thy wings a place.
Lest we lose this day of grace
Ere we shall behold Thy Face. — Amen.

175

Love Divine, all love excelling,
  Joy of Heaven, to earth come down!
Fix in us Thy humble dwelling,
  All Thy faithful mercies crown.
Jesus, Thou art all compassion,
  Pure, unbounded love Thou art;
Visit us with Thy salvation,
  Enter every trembling heart.

Breathe, O breathe Thy loving Spirit
  Into every troubled breast!
Let us all in Thee inherit,
  Let us find Thy promised rest;
Take away the love of sinning,
  Alpha and Omega be,—
End of faith, as its beginning,
  Set our hearts at liberty.

Come, Almighty to deliver,
  Let us all Thy grace receive;
Suddenly return, and never,
  Never more Thy temples leave.

Thee we would be always blessing;
 Serve Thee as Thy hosts above;
Pray, and praise Thee without ceasing;
 Glory in Thy perfect love.

Finish then Thy new creation,
 Pure and spotless let us be:
Let us see Thy great salvation,
 Perfectly restored in Thee.
Changed from glory into glory,
 Till in Heaven we take ourplace;
Till we cast our crowns before Thee,
 Lost in wonder, love, and praise.
    —Amen.

176

The Royal Banners forward go,
The Cross shines forth in mystic glow;
Where He in Flesh, our flesh Who made,
Our sentence bore, our ransom paid,

There whilst He hung, His sacred Side
By soldier's spear was opened wide,
To cleanse us in the precious flood
Of Water mingled with His Blood.

Fulfilled is now what David told
In true prophetic song of old,
How GOD the heathen's King should be;
For GOD is reigning from the Tree.

O Tree of glory, Tree most fair,
Ordained those Holy Limbs to bear,
How bright in purple robe it stood,
The purple of a Saviour's Blood!

Upon its arms, like balance true,
He weighed the price for sinners due,
The price which none but He could pay,
And spoiled the spoiler of his prey.

To Thee, Eternal THREE in ONE,
Let homage meet by all be done:
As by the Cross Thou dost restore,
So rule and guide us evermore.—Amen.

177

Weary of earth and laden with my sin,
I look at heaven and long to enter in;
But there no evil thing may find a home,
And yet I hear a voice that bids me,
  "Come."

So vile I am, how dare I hope to stand
In the pure glory of that holy land?
Before the whiteness of that Throne appear?
Yet there are Hands stretched out to draw me near.

The while I fain would tread the heavenly way,
Evil is ever with me day by day;
Yet on mine ears the gracious tidings fall,
"Repent, confess, thou shall be loosed from all."

It is the voice of JESUS that I hear,
His are the Hands stretched out to draw me near,
And His the Blood that can for all atone,
And set me faultless there before the Throne.

"Twas He Who found me on the deathly wild,
And made me heir of heaven, the FATHER's child,

And day by day, whereby my soul may
    live,
Gives me His grace of pardon, and will
    give.

O great Absolver, grant my soul may
    wear
The lowliest garb of penitence and prayer,
That in the FATHER'S courts my glori-
    ous dress
May be the garment of Thy righteous-
    ness.

Yea, Thou wilt answer for me, Right-
    eous LORD;
Thine all the merits, mine the great re-
    ward;
Thine the sharp thorns, and mine the
    golden crown;
Mine the life won, and Thine the life
    laid down.

Nought can I bring, dear LORD, for all
    I owe,
Yet let my full heart what it can bestow:
Like Mary's gift let my devotion prove,
Forgiven greatly, how I greatly love.
                        Amen.

178

CHRIST the LORD is risen to-day,
Sons of men and angels say:
Raise your joys and triumphs high,
Sing, ye heavens; and earth, reply.

Love's redeeming work is done,
Fought the fight, the victory won:
JESUS' agony is o'er,
Darkness veils the earth no more.

Vain the stone, the watch, the seal,
CHRIST hath burst the gates of hell;
Death in vain forbids Him rise,
CHRIST hath open'd Paradise.

Soar we now where CHRIST hath led,
Following our exalted Head;
Made like Him, like Him we rise:
Ours the cross, the grave, the skies.
—Amen.

179

GOD the FATHER, GOD the SON,
GOD the SPIRIT, THREE in ONE,
Hear us from Thy heavenly Throne,
    Spare us, Holy TRINITY.

Thou Who leaving Crown and Throne
Camest here, an outcast lone,
That Thou mightest save Thine own,
    Hear us, Holy JESU.

Thou with sinners wont to eat,
Who with loving Words didst greet
Mary weeping at Thy Feet,
    Hear us, Holy JESU.

Thou Whose saddened look did chide
Peter when he thrice denied,
Till with bitter tears he cried,
    Hear us, Holy JESU.

Thou Who hanging on the Tree
To the thief saidst, "Thou shalt be
To-day in Paradise with Me,"
    Hear us, Holy JESU.

Thou, despised, denied, refused,
And for man's transgressions bruised,
Sinless, yet of sin accused,
    Hear us, Holy JESU.

Thou, Who on the Cross didst reign,
Dying there in bitter pain,
Cleansing with Thy Blood our stain,
  Hear us, Holy JESU.

Shepherd of the straying sheep,
Comforter of them that weep,
Hear us crying from the deep,
  Hear us, Holy JESU.

That in Thy pure innocence
We may wash our souls' offence,
And find truest penitence.
  We beseech Thee, JESU.

That we give to sin no place,
That we never quench Thy grace,
That we ever seek Thy Face,
  We beseech Thee, JESU.

That denying evil lust,
Living godly, meek, and just,
In Thee only we may trust,
  We beseech Thee, JESU.

That to sin for ever dead
We may live to Thee instead,
And the narrow pathway tread,
  We beseech Thee, JESU.

When shall end the battle sore,
When our Pilgrimage is o'er,
Grant Thy peace for evermore,
  We beseech Thee, JESU.
     —Amen.

180

PART I.

 Faithful Shepherd of Thine own,
 Unto Whom each sheep is known,

Low before Thine Altar Throne,
  We adore Thee, JESU.

O how blest to draw so near,
Unto Thee, our Saviour dear,
Who in mystery art here;
  And adore Thee, JESU.

Thou who tenderly hast smiled,
As a little helpless Child,
On Thy Maiden-Mother mild;
  Hear us, save us, JESU.

Whom the star-led Magi three,
Came from far off lands to see,
Whom they worshipped reverently;
  Hear us, save us, JESU.

Kneeling in the stable cave,
Incense, myrrh, and gold they gave,
We would offer all we have;
  Hear, accept us, JESU.

As in worship low, we kneel,
May we Thy sweet Presence feel!
All Thy love to us reveal;
  Hear, accept us. JESU.

181

PART II.

Faithful Shepherd hear our cry,
To Thine arms Thy lambs would fly,
On Thy boundless love rely;
  Hear us, save us, JESU.

Lamb of God Who takest away
All our sin, on Thee we lay
Every sin and grief to-day;
  Hear us, save us, JESU.

Thou all sinless, holy, pure.
For our sins didst grief endure.
Thou hast made our pardon sure ;
    Hear us, save us. JESU.

Sorrow for our sins impart,
Cleanse and soften every heart,
In Thy merits give us part ;
    Hear us, save us, JESU.

By Thy grace within us shed,
May our youthful feet be led,
Paths of holiness to tread :
    Hear us, save us, JESU.

182

PART III.

Shepherd, Who Thy life didst give,
That Thy sheep in Thee might live.
Now our grateful praise receive,
    Hear, accept us, JESU.

As 'neath veils of bread and wine,
We adore Thee, King Divine,
Make Thy Face upon us shine ;
    Hear, accept us, JESU.

May our lips and lives express,
Faith and love, and thankfulness,
Fill us with all holiness :
    Hear, accept us, JESU.

Make us love Thee more and more,
Till we reach the Eternal shore,
Where unveiled evermore,
    We behold Thee, JESU.

Then in worship falling down,
Low before Thy Glory Throne,
We shall know as we are known,
    Praise, exalt Thee, JESU.
        —Amen.

183

Forward! Forward, Christians,
   Forward to the fight,
For the law of JESUS,
   For the Gospel-light;
'Tis no time to dally,
   'Tis no time to wait,
When the hosts of evil
   Thunder at the gate.

   Forward! Forward, Christians,
     Forward! to the fight,
   For the love of JESUS,
     For the Church's right.

Ask they what we fight for!
   'Tis the blessed CHRIST—
Present really, truly,
   In His Eucharist;
Come, let us adore Him,
   Let us bow the knee;
King, He claims our worship,
   Claims our fealty.
     Forward! Forward, etc.

Fearful was the anguish,
   Which for us He bore,
Ere the work was finished,
   And the struggle o'er;
Life of lowly labor,
   Horrors of the grave;
This the dread atonement,
   This the price He gave.
     Forward! Forward, etc.

On the eve of Passion,
   With His Church was He,
When the shades were falling
   On Gethsemane;

Then that Gift was given
  Which we love so well,—
God-with-us forever,
  CHRIST, EMMANUEL.

    Forward! Forward, etc.

Shall we slight that Presence?
  Shall we CHRIST deny?
Shall we stint our worship,
  When He draweth nigh?
GOD in Heaven forbid it!
  GOD attest our word,—
We will worship JESUS,
  We will serve the LORD.

    Forward! Forward, etc.

Now to GOD the FATHER,
  Now to GOD the SON,
To the Blessed SPIRIT,
  To the Three in One,
Give we praise and honor,
  As we vow to fight
For the love of JÉSUS,
  For the Gospel-light—

    Foward! Forward, etc.—Amen.

184

Christian, dost thou see them,
  On the holy ground,
How the troops of Midian
  Prowl and prowl around?
Christian, up and smite them,
  Counting gain but loss;
Smite them by the merit
  Of the holy Cross.

Christian, dost thou feel them,
   How they work within,
Striving, tempting, luring,
   Goading into sin?
Christian, never tremble:
   Never be down-cast;
Smite them by the virtue
   Of the Lenten fast.

Christian, dost thou hear them,
   How they speak thee fair?
"Always fast and vigil?
   Always watch and prayer?"
Christian, answer boldly,
   "While I breathe I pray:"
Peace shall follow battle,
   Night shall end in day.

"Well I know thy trouble,
   O My servant true;
Thou art very weary,
   I was weary too;
But that toil shall make thee
   Some day all Mine own,
And the end of sorrow
   Shall be near My Throne."—Amen.

185

Blessed feasts of Blessed Martyrs,
   Holy days of Holy men,
With affection's recollections,
   Greet we your return again.
Worthy deeds they wrought and wonders,
   Worthy of the Name they bore;
We with meetest praise and sweetest
   Honour them for evermore.

Faith prevailing, hope unfailing,
    JESUS loved with single heart—
Thus they glorious and victorious
    Bravely bore the Martyr's part.
Racked with torture, haled to slaughter,
    Fire, and axe, and murderous sword,
Chains and prison, foes' derision
    They endured for CHRIST the LORD.

So they passed through pain and sorrow,
    Till they sank in death to rest;
Earth's rejected, GOD's elected,
    Gained a portion with the blest.
By contempt of worldly pleasures,
    And by deeds of valour done,
They have reached the land of Angels,
    And with them are knit in one.

Made co-heirs with CHRIST in glory,
    His celestial bliss they share:
May they now before Him bending
    Help us onward by their prayer;
That, this weary life completed,
    And its fleeting trials past,
We may win eternal glory
    In our FATHER's home at last.—Amen.

186

Draw nigh and take the Body of the LORD,
And drink the holy Blood for you out-
    poured.
Saved by that Body and that holy Blood,
With souls refreshed, we tender thanks
    to GOD.
Salvation's Giver, CHRIST, the Only SON,
By His dear Cross and Blood the victory
    won.

Offered was He for greatest and for least,
Himself the Victim, and Himself the
    Priest.
Victims were offered by the law of old,
Which in a type this heavenly mystery
    told.
He Ransomer from death, and Light
    from shade,
Now gives His Holy grace His saints to
    aid.
Approach ye then with faithful hearts
    sincere,
And take the safeguard of salvation here.
He, that His saints in this world rules
    and shields,
To all believers life eternal yields;
With heavenly bread makes them that
    hunger whole,
Gives living waters to the thirsting soul.
Alpha and Omega, to Whom shall bow
All nations at the Doom, is with us now.
                   —Amen

187

Sing Alleluia forth in duteous praise,
Ye citizens of Heaven; O sweetly raise
        An endless Alleluia.
Ye Powers, who stand before the Eternal
    Light,
In hymning choirs re-echo to the height
        An endless Alleluia.
The Holy City shall take up your strain,
And with glad songs resounding wake
    again
        An endless Alleluia.

In blissful antiphons ye thus rejoice
To render to the LORD with thankful voice
    An endless Alleluia.
Ye who have gained at length your palms in bliss,
Victorious ones, your chant shall still be this,
    An endless Alleluia.
There, in one glad acclaim, for ever ring
The strains which tell the honour of your King,
    An endless Alleluia
This is sweet rest for weary ones brought back,
This is glad food and drink which ne'er shall lack,
    An endless Alleluia.
While Thee, by Whom were all things made, we praise
For ever, and tell out in sweetest lays
    An endless Alleluia.
Almighty CHRIST, to Thee our voices sing
Glory for evermore; to Thee we bring
    An endless Alleluia.—Amen.

188

Behold a humble train
  The courts of GOD draw near;
A Virgin Mother and her Babe
  Before the LORD appear.

O wondrous, blessed sight!
  To faithful eyes made known,
That lowly Babe—the mighty GOD,
  The Prince of Peace, they own.

And now this temple shines
   With glory far more bright,
Than e'er the former temple saw,
   E'en at its greatest height.

The cloud indeed was there,
   The symbol of the LORD;
But here the LORD Himself appears,
   The true, incarnate Word.

Blest SAVIOUR, come once more
   With power and grace divine;
Our hearts Thy living temples make,
   Wholly and ever Thine.—Amen.

189

The GOD of Abraham praise,
   Who reigns enthroned above;
Ancient of everlasting days,
   And GOD of love:
JEHOVAH, great I AM,
   By earth and Heaven confessed;—
I bow and bless the sacred Name,
   For ever blessed.

The GOD of Abraham praise,
   At Whose supreme command
From earth I rise, and seek the joys
   At His right hand:
I all on earth forsake,
Its wisdom, fame, and power;
And Him my only portion make,
   My shield and tower.

He by Himself hath sworn,
   I on His oath depend,
I shall, on angel-wings upborne,
   To heaven ascend:

I shall behold His face,
I shall His power adore,
And sing the wonders of His grace
For evermore.

There dwells the LORD, our King,
The LORD, our righteousness,
Triumphant o'er the world and sin,
The Prince of Peace:
On Sion's sacred height
His kingdom He maintains,
And glorious with His Saints in light
For ever reigns.

The GOD Who reigns on high
The great archangels sing:
And, "Holy, holy, holy," cry,
"Almighty King,
Who was, and is the same,
And evermore shall be ;.
JEHOVAH, FATHER, great I AM,
We worship thee."

The whole triumphant host
Give thanks to GOD on high ;
Hail, FATHER, SON, and HOLY GHOST,
They ever cry ;
Hail, Abraham's GOD and mine,
I join the heavenly lays ;
All might and majesty are Thine,
And endless praise.—Amen.

190

Look, ye Saints; the sight is glorious ;
See the "Man of Sorrows" now :
From the fight returned victorious,
Every knee to Him shall bow :
Crown Him ! Crown Him !
Crowns become the Victor's brow.

Crown the SAVIOUR, angels crown Him;
 Rich the trophies JESUS brings;
On the seat of power enthrone Him,
 While the vault of heaven rings;
  Crown Him! Crown Him!
 Crown the SAVIOUR King of kings.

Sinners in derision crowned Him,
 Mocking thus the SAVIOUR'S claim;
Saints and Angels crowd around Him,
 Own His title, praise His name;
  Crown Him! Crown Him!
 Spread abroad the Victor's fame!

Hark! those bursts of acclamation!
 Hark! those loud triumphant chords!
JESUS takes the highest station;
 O what joy the sight affords!
  Crown Him! Crown Him!
 King of kings, and LORD of lords.
          —Amen.

191

Chorus.
Shout the glad tidings, exultingly sing;
Jerusalem triumphs, MESSIAH is King!

'Sion, the marvellous story be telling,
 The SON of the Highest, how lowly
   His birth!
The brightest archangel in glory excelling,
 He stoops to redeem them, He reigns
   upon earth:

Cho.—Shout the glad tidings, &c.

Tell how He cometh; from nation to
   nation,
 The heart-cheering news let the earth
   echo round:

(175)

How free to the faithful he offers salvation,
  How His people with joy everlasting are crown'd :

Cho.—Shout the glad tidings, &c.

Mortals, your homage be gratefully bringing,
  And sweet let the gladsome Hosanna arise ;
Ye angels the full Hallelujah be singing;
  One chorus resound through the earth and the skies :

Cho.—Shout the glad tidings, &c.

192

Holy, holy, holy. Lord
  God of hosts, eternal King,
By the heavens and earth adored :
  Angels and Archangels sing,
Chanting everlastingly
To the Blessed Trinity.

Thousands, tens of thousands, stand,
  Spirits blest, before Thy throne,
Speeding thence at Thy command ;
  And when Thy command is done,
Singing everlastingly
To the Blessed Trinity.

Cherubim and Seraphim
  Veil their faces with their wings ;
Eyes of Angels are too dim
  To behold the King of kings,
While they sing eternally
To the Blessed Trinity.

Thee, apostles, prophets, Thee,
 Thee, the noble martyr band,
Praise with solemn jubilee;
 Thee the Church in every land:
Singing everlastingly
To the Blessed TRINITY.

Alleluia! LORD, to Thee,
 FATHER, SON, and HOLY GHOST,
THREE in ONE, and ONE in THREE.
 Join we with the heavenly host,
Singing everlastingly
To the Blessed TRINITY.—Amen.

193

When GOD of old came down from heaven,
 In power and wrath He came;
Before His feet the clouds were riven,
 Half darkness and half flame.

But, when He came the second time,
 He came in power and love;
Softer than gale at morning prime
 Hovered His holy Dove.

The fires, that rushed on Sinai down
 In sudden torrents dread,
Now gently light, a glorious crown,
 On every sainted head.

And as on Israel's awe-struck ear
 The voice exceeding loud,
The trump, that Angels quake to hear,
 Thrilled from the deep, dark cloud;

So, when the SPIRIT of our GOD
 Came down His flock to find,
A voice from heaven was heard abroad,
 A rushing, mighty wind.

It fills the Church of GOD ; It fills
    The sinful world around ;
Only in stubborn hearts and wills
    No place for It is found

Come LORD, come Wisdom, Love, and
        Power,
    Open our ears to hear ;
Let us not miss the accepted hour ;
    Save, LORD, by love or fear.—Amen.

194

On the Resurrection morning
    Soul and body meet again ;
No more sorrow, no more weeping,
        No more pain.

Here awhile they must be parted,
    And the flesh its Sabbath keep,
Waiting in a holy stillness—
        Wrapt in sleep.

For a space the tired body
    Lies with feet toward the dawn,
Till there breaks the last and brightest
        Easter morn.

But thy soul in contemplation
    Utters earnest prayer and strong,
Breaking at the Resurrection
        Into song.

Soul and body reunited,
    Thenceforth nothing shall divide ;
Waking up in CHRIST's own likeness,
        Satisfied.

Oh, the beauty ! Oh, the gladness
    Of that Resurrection day !
Which shall not, thro' endless ages,
        Pass away.

On that happy Easter morning
    All the graves their dead restore.
Father, sister, child and mother
            Meet once more

To that brightest of all meetings,
    Bring us, JESUS CHRIST, at last;
To Thy Cross, thro' death and judgment,
            Holding fast.—Amen.

195

O Word of GOD above,
    Who fillest all in all,
Hallow this House with Thy sure love,
    And bless our festival

Here from the Font is poured
    Grace on each guilty child;
The blest anointing of the LORD
    Brightens the once defiled.

Here CHRIST to faithful hearts
    His Body gives for Food;
The Lamb of GOD Himself imparts
    The Chalice of His Blood.

Here guilty souls that pine
    May health and pardon win;
The Judge acquits, and grace divine
    Restores the dead in sin.

Yea, GOD enthroned on high
    Here also dwells to bless·
Here trains adoring souls that sigh
    His mansions to possess.

Against this holy Home
    Rude tempests harmless beat,
And Satan's angels fiercely come,
    But to endure defeat.—Amen.

196

Good it is to keep the fast,
Shadowed forth in ages past.
Which our own Almighty LORD
Hallowed by His Deed and Word.

Moses, while he fasted, saw
GOD, Who gave by him the Law:
To Elijah Angels came,
Steeds of fire and car of flame:

So was Daniel meet to gaze
On the sight of latter days,
And the Baptist to proclaim
Blessings thro' the Bridegroom's Name.

Grant us, LORD, like them to be
Oft in prayer and fast with Thee;
Fill us with Thy heavenly might,
Be our joy and true delight.

FATHER, hear us through Thy SON
And the SPIRIT, with Thee ONE,
Whom our thankful hearts adore
Ever and forevermore.—Amen.

197

Thou art coming, O my SAVIOUR,
  Thou art coming, O my King,
In Thy beauty all-resplendent,
In Thy glory all-transcendent,
  Well may we rejoice and sing;
Coming! in the opening east,
  Herald brightness slowly swells;
Coming! O my glorious Priest,
  Hear we not Thy golden bells?

Thou art coming, Thou art coming;
  We shall meet Thee on Thy way,
We shall see Thee, we shall know Thee,

We shall bless Thee, we shall show Thee
   All our hearts could never say:
What an anthem that will be
   Ringing out our love to Thee,
Pouring out our rapture sweet
   At Thine own all-glorious Feet.

Thou art coming; at Thy Table
   We are witnesses for this;
While remembering hearts Thou meetest
In communion clearest, sweetest,
   Earnest of our coming bliss;
Showing not Thy death alone,
   And Thy love exceeding great,
But Thy coming, and Thy Throne,
   All for which we long and wait.

Thou art coming; we are waiting
   With a hope that cannot fail.
Asking not the day or hour,
Resting on Thy Word of power
   Anchored safe within the veil.
Time appointed may be long,
   But the Vision must be sure;
Certainty shall make us strong,
   Joyful patience can endure.

O, the joy to see Thee reigning.
   Thee, my own beloved LORD!
Every tongue Thy Name confessing,
Worship, honor, glory, blessing,
   Brought to Thee with one accord
Thee my Master and my Friend.
   Vindicated and enthroned,
Unto earth's remotest end
   Glorified, adored, and owned!—Amen.

198

I love the holy Angels,
   So beautiful and bright,

And, though I cannot see them,
   They're with me day and night;
They watch around my bedside,
   They see me at my play,
They know my every action,
   They hear the words I say.

'Tis GOD our Heavenly Father,
   Who doth the Angels send,
To guard His little children,
   Until their life shall end;
When I am cross and naughty,
   The holy Angels grieve;
For they are sad when children
   The way of goodness leave.

And when I die, the Angels
   Will bear my soul away,
While here my body resteth
   Until the judgment day:
They'll bear me gently, softly,
   With loving care most sweet,
And lay me down in safety
   At my Redeemer's feet.

At last, with Blessed Spirits,
   And holy men of old,
And all good friends who love me,
   Too many to be told,
I shall be—with the Angels
   And all that people bright—
For ever, and for ever,
   In GOD's most glorious light.—Amen

199

   O worship JESUS now,
      For He is here!
   Before His Altar bow,
      For He is here!
   The Lamb of GOD once slain,

Is offered now again,
Pleading for sinful men:
  JESUS is here!

Angels are kneeling round.
  For He is here!
They guard this Holy Ground,
  For He is here!
And even children dare
A feeble part to bear,
And in their praise to share;
  JESUS is here!

We hear His Voice so blest.
  For He is here!
Stilling our hearts to rest,
  For He is here!
Before His Altar Throne,
Lay every burden down,
And every need make known;
  JESUS is here!

Then worship and adore,
  For He is here!
Then love Him more and more.
  For He is here!
O Feast of priceless worth!
The SAVIOUR's death shown forth!
Yes, this is Heaven on earth!
  JESUS is here!—Amen.

200

At the Name of JESUS,
  Every knee shall bow,
Every tongue confess Him
  King of glory now:

'Tis the FATHER's pleasure
  We should call Him LORD,
Who from the beginning
  Was the Mighty WORD.

At His voice creation
  Sprang at once to sight,
All the Angel faces,
  All the hosts of light,
Thrones and Dominations,
  Stars upon their way,
All the heavenly Orders
  In their great array.

Humbled for a season,
  To receive a Name
From the lips of sinners
  Unto whom He came.
Faithfully He bore it
  Spotless to the last,
Brought it back victorious,
  When from death He passed:

Bore it up triumphant,
  With its human light,
Through all ranks of creatures,
  To the central height;
To the Throne of GODHEAD,
  To the FATHER's breast,
Filled it with the glory
  Of that perfect rest.

In your hearts enthrone Him;
  There let Him subdue
All that is not holy,
  All that is not true:

Crown Him as your Captain
  In temptation's hour;
Let His will enfold you
  In its light and power.

Brothers, this LORD JESUS
  Shall return again,
With His FATHER's glory,
  With His Angel train;
For all wreaths of empire
  Meet upon His Brow,
And our hearts confess Him
  King of glory now.—Amen.

201

Let saints on earth in concert sing
  With those whose work is done:
For all the servants of our King
  In Heaven and earth are one.

One family, we dwell in Him,
  One Church, above, beneath;
Though now divided by the stream,
  The narrow stream of death.

One army of the living GOD,
  To His command we bow;
Part of the host have crossed the flood;
  And part are crossing now.

E'en now to their eternal home
  There pass some spirits blest;
While others to the margin come,
  Waiting their call to rest.

JESU, be Thou our constant Guide;
  Then, when the word is given,
Bid Jordan's narrow stream divide,
  And bring us safe to Heaven.—Amen.

202

As we tread life's weary journey,
  All we suffer on the way,
We will offer up to Jesus,
  And with hearts submissive say—

"All for Jesus! what we suffer
  He has suffered long before,
Each dear cross we bear behind Him
  Shall but make us love Him more."

If it is our lot to labour,
  And with toil we feel oppressed;
We will think of Him who laboured
  That our labours might be blessed.
    "All for Jesus," &c.

When temptations try us sorely,
  We shall more than conquerors be,
Wrestling as our Saviour wrestled,
  Prostrate in Gethsemane.
    "All for Jesus," &c.

Death for us shall have no terrors,
  He has robbed it of its sting:
Through its gloom He bids us follow
  To the Palace of our King.
    "All for Jesus," &c.—Amen.

203

Lord, speak to me, that I may speak
  In living echoes of Thy tone;
As Thou hast sought, so let me seek
  Thy erring children lost and lone.

O lead me, Lord, that I may lead
  The wandering and the wavering feet;
O feed me, Lord, that I may feed
  Thy hungering ones with manna sweet.

O strengthen me, that while I stand
   Firm on the Rock and strong in Thee,
I may stretch out a loving hand
   To wrestlers with the troubled sea

O teach me, LORD, that I may teach
   The precious things Thou dost impart;
And wing my words, that they may reach
   The hidden depths of many a heart.

O give Thine own sweet rest to me,
   That I may speak with soothing power
A word in season, as from Thee,
   To weary ones in needful hour.

O fill me with Thy fulness, LORD,
   Until my very heart o'erflow
In kindling thought and glowing word,
   Thy love to tell, Thy praise to show.

O use me, LORD, use even me,
Just as Thou wilt, and when, and where;
Until Thy Blessed Face I see,
   Thy rest, Thy joy, Thy glory share.
                   —Amen.

204

There is a Fountain filled with Blood
   Drawn from Emmanuel's veins,
And sinners plunged beneath that Flood
   Lose all their guilty stains.
The dying thief rejoiced to see
   That Fountain opened wide,
And now may I as well as he
   Be cleansed beneath its tide.

   I do believe, I will believe,
      That JESUS died for me,
   That on the cross He shed His Blood
      From sin to set me free.

The Precious Blood! O how it wrought
   That Pentecostal day,
When sinners first in Baptism
   Washed all their sins away.
Converted Saul received his sight
   And heard the Prophet say,
"Brother arise, and be baptised
   And wash thy sins away."
     I do believe, &c.

The Precious Blood! O how it comes
   To set the sinner free,
When CHRIST by priestly voice transmits
   His word "I pardon thee,"
When Corinth's sinner steeped in crime,
   Repenting, heard Paul's word,
"In CHRIST's own Person I forgive,"
   He was to grace restored.
     I do believe, &c.

Dear Dying Lamb, Thy Precious Blood
   Shall never lose its power,
Till all the ransomed Church of GOD
   Be saved to sin no more.
'Twas death to him who drank of old
   The blood of victims shed;
'Tis life to taste the Blood of CHRIST;
   For so Himself hath said.
     I do delieve, &c.

Now since by grace, I've found the stream
   Which flows from out Thy Side,
My guilty soul, absolved and freed,
   Shall praise the Crucified.
And in a nobler, sweeter song,
   I'll sing Thy power to save,   [tongue
When this poor lisping stammering
   Lies silent in the grave.
     I do believe, &c.

Lord I believe Thou hast prepared,
   Unworthy though I be,
For me a Blood-bought free reward.
   A golden harp for me.
'Tis strung and tuned for endless years.
   And formed by power Divine,
To sound in God the Father's ears
   No other name but Thine.
   I do believe, &c.   —Amen.

205

The Church is my Mother, I owe her my love,
The Catholic Church of CHRIST JESUS above,
Of old Eve was Mother of all sons of earth;
Now God gives another by heavenly birth.

   The Church, &c.

Ere JESUS ascended in that parting hour
He gave His commission investing with power,
"Go forth to the nations and teach in My Name,
And lo! I am with you, till earth ends in flame.

   The Church, &c.

O Church of the SAVIOUR, by promise secure,
Though winds whistle chilly and wither thy leaf,
Our love for thee, Mother, shall grow with thy grief.

   The Church, &c.

Then those that are faithful, that hold
  to thee fast,
Shall shine in thy splendor, in Heaven at
  last;
For CHRIST in His glory shall summon
  His Bride
To share in His triumph and reign at
  His Side.
   The Church, &c. —Amen.

206

The Church! the Church! the Holy
  My fathers' and my own! [Church!
On Prophets and Apostles built,
  And CHRIST the Corner-stone.
Upon this Rock 'gainst every shock,
  Though gates of Hell assail,
She stands secure with promise sure—
  "They never shall prevail."

The Church! the Church! the Holy
  When to the font I came, [Church!
She took me in her loving arms,
  And gave me my new name. [seek,
When faint and weak, fresh strength I
  She brings me Bread from Heaven,
That Heavenly Food, that precious Blood
  Whereby new life is given.

The Church! the Church! the Holy
  My SAVIOUR holds so dear, [Church!
In His own Name she speaks, she guides,
  Let none refuse to hear;
And when her voice bids me rejoice,
  From all my sins released,
It is my LORD that speaks the word,
  Through His appointed Priest.

The Church! the Church! I love the
    For she doth lead me on,   [Church!
Unto that bright, eternal Home,
    Where many a saint has gone;
And when I go from strife and woe
    To rest in peace and love,
I shall but leave the Church below,
    To join the Church above.

The Church! the Church! the Holy
    Thy child would add this vow   [Church!
To those he made when first the Cross
    Was signed upon his brow:
Assault who may, fail or betray,
    Dishonor or disown,
The Church shall still be dear to me,
    Her faith shall be my own.—Amen.

207

Fling out the banner! let it float
    Skyward and seaward, high and wide;
The sun that lights its shining folds,
    The Cross on which the SAVIOUR died.

Fling out the banner! Angels bend
    In anxious silence o'er the Sign,
And vainly seek to comprehend
    The wonder of the Love Divine.

Fling out the banner! Heathen lands
    Shall see from far the glorious sight,
And nations, gathering at the call,
    Their spirits kindle in its light.

Fling out the banner! Sin-sick souls,
    That sink and perish in the strife,
Shall touch in faith its radiant hems,
    And spring immortal into life.

Fling out the banner! let it float
  Skyward and seaward, high and wide;
Our glory only in the Cross,
  Our only hope, the Crucified.

Fling out the banner! wide and high,
  Seaward and skyward, let it shine;
Nor skill, nor might, nor merit ours;
  We conquer only in the Sign.—Amen.

208

O Word of God Incarnate,
  O Wisdom from on high,
O Truth unchanged, unchanging,
  O Light of our dark sky;
We praise Thee for the radiance
  That from the hallowed page,
A lantern to our footsteps,
  Shines on from age to age.

The Church from her dear Master
  Received the gift divine,
And still that light she lifteth
  O'er all the earth to shine.
It is the golden casket
  Where gems of truth are stored;
It is the heaven-drawn picture
  Of Christ the living Word.

It floateth like a banner
  Before God's host unfurled;
It shineth like a beacon
  Above the darkling world;
It is the chart and compass
  That o'er life's surging sea,
Mid mists and rocks and quicksands,
  Still guides, O Christ to Thee.

O make Thy Church, dear SAVIOUR,
  A lamp of burnished gold,
To bear before the nations
  Thy true Light as of old ;
O teach Thy wandering pilgrims
  By this their path to trace,
Till, clouds and darkness ended,
  They see Thee Face to face.—Amen,

209

Jesus, Master, King of Glory,
  Still to Thee we turn for life;
Conqueror when the battle's sorest,
  O sustain us in the strife.

When the World is hard upon us,
  And we flinch before its scorn,
Let us learn an earnest purpose
  From Thy Forehead pierced with thorn.
    Jesus, Master, etc.

When the Flesh is strong and round us
  All its poisonous vapors roll,
By Thy lacerated Body,
  Dear Redeemer, save the soul.
    Jesus, Master, etc.

When the Fiend with subtlest temptings
  Lures us to our endless loss,
Mighty Master, strike the strong one
  With the sharpness of Thy Cross.
    Jesus, Master, etc.

When the last dark storm is gathering,
  And our hearts are swept with fear,
By the love of Thy dear Passion,
  Master, let us feel Thee near.
    Jesus, Master, etc.

So when all at last is ended,
   And the Rest is reached above;
May we swell Thy Heart's rejoicings
   With the rapture of our love.
      JESUS, Master, etc.   —Amen.

210

At even ere the sun was set,
The sick, O LORD, around Thee lay;
Oh, in what divers pain they met!
Oh, with what joy they went away!

Once more 'tis eventide, and we
Oppressed with various ills draw near;
What if Thy Form we cannot see?
We know and feel that Thou art here.

O Saviour CHRIST, our woes dispel;
For some are sick, and some are sad,
And some have never loved Thee well,
And some have lost the love they had;

And some have found the world is vain,
Yet from the world they break not free;
And some have friends who give them pain,
Yet have not sought a friend in Thee·

And none, O LORD, have perfect rest,
For none are wholly free from sin;
And they, who fain would serve Thee best,
Are conscious most of wrong within.

O Saviour CHRIST, Thou too art Man;
Thou hast been troubled, tempted, tried;
Thy kind but searching glance can scan
The very wounds that shame would hide;

(194)

Thy touch has still its ancient power;
No word from Thee can fruitless fall;
Hear, in this solemn evening hour,
And in Thy mercy heal us all.—Amen.

211

If I could be an Angel,
  And with the Angels stand,
A crown upon my forehead,
  A harp within my hand:
O then before my SAVIOUR,
  So glorious and so bright,
I'd raise the sweetest music
  And praise Him day and night.

I never should be weary,
  Nor ever shed a tear,
Nor ever know a sorrow,
  Nor ever feel a fear;
But blessed pure and holy:
  I'd dwell in JESUS' sight,
And with ten thousand thousands,
  Praise Him both day and night.

I cannot be an Angel
  And yet I hope to stand,
With all the saints of JESUS,
  One day at His right Hand;
O then before my SAVIOUR,
  So glorious and so bright.
I'll join the shining Angels,
  And praise Him day and night.

I know I'm weak and sinful,
  But JESUS can forgive,
And so with Him forever
  I hope in Heaven to live.

Dear SAVIOUR, when I languish,
  And lay me down to die,
O send the shining Angels
  To bear me up on high.—Amen.

212

Come, Thou Almighty King,
Help us Thy name to sing,
  Help us to praise!
Father all glorious,
O'er all victorious,
Come and reign over us,
  Ancient of days.

Come, Thou incarnate Word,
Gird on Thy mighty sword;
  Our prayer attend;
Come, and Thy people bless;
Come, give Thy Word success,
Spirit of holiness,
  On us descend!

Come, Holy Comforter,
Thy sacred witness bear,
  In this glad hour;
Thou, Who almighty art,
Now rule in every heart,
And ne'er from us depart,
  Spirit of power.

To Thee, great ONE in THREE,
The highest praises be,
  Hence evermore;
Thy sovereign majesty
May we in glory see,
And to eternity,
  Love and adore.—Amen.

213

Blessed city, heavenly Salem,
   Vision dear of peace and love,
Who of living stones are builded
   In the height of Heaven above,
And, with Angel hosts encircled,
   As a bride doth earthward move:

From celestial realms descending,
   Bridal glory round thee shed,
Meet for Him Whose love espoused thee,
   To thy LORD shalt thou be led;
All thy streets and all thy bulwarks
   Of pure gold are fashioned.

Bright thy gates of pearl are shining,
   They are open evermore;
And by virtue of His merits
   Thither faithful souls do soar,
Who for CHRIST's dear Name in this world
   Pain and tribulation bore.

Many a blow and biting sculpture
   Polished well those stones elect,
In their places now compacted
   By the heavenly Architect,
Who therewith hath willed for ever
   That His Palace should be decked.

214

PART 2.

CHRIST is made the sure Foundation,
   CHRIST the Head and Corner-stone,
Chosen of the LORD, and precious,
   Binding all the Church in one,
Holy Sion's help for ever,
   And her confidence alone.

All that dedicated city,
  Dearly loved of GOD on high,
In exultant jubilation
  Pours perpetual melody,
GOD the ONE in THREE adoring
  In glad hymns eternally.

To this temple, where we call Thee,
  Come, O LORD of hosts, to-day;
With Thy wonted loving-kindness
  Hear Thy servants, as they pray;
And Thy fullest benediction
  Shed within its walls alway.

Here vouchsafe to all Thy servants
  What they ask of Thee to gain,
What they gain from Thee for ever
  With the Blessed to retain,
And hereafter in Thy glory
  Evermore with Thee to reign.

DOXOLOGY FOR EACH PART.

Laud and honour to the FATHER,
  Laud and honour to the SON,
Laud and honour to the SPIRIT,
  Ever THREE, and ever ONE,
Consubstantial, Co-eternal,
  While unending ages run.—Amen.

215

FATHER, from Thy Throne on high,
Deign to hear Thy children's cry,
Let them feel that Thou art nigh;
      We beseech Thee, hear us.

FATHER, Thou dost love us all,
And we come at Thy dear call,
Low before Thy Feet to fall;
  We beseech Thee, hear us.

JESU, tender Shepherd, hear;
Bid Thy little ones draw near;
Train them to Thy love and fear;
  We beseech Thee, hear us.

By the promise Thou hast made,
By Thy Hands in blessing laid,
By the words that Thou hast said;
  We beseech Thee, hear us.

Weak and helpless, LORD are we,
Yet Thy love is all our plea.
Suffer us to come to Thee;
  We beseech Thee, hear us.

HOLY SPIRIT, Guide Divine,
Let Thy Light for ever shine,
Leave us not, for we are Thine;
  We beseech Thee, hear us.

'Neath Thy Wings, O blessed Dove,
May we feel Thy sheltering love,
Til we reach our home above;
  We beseech Thee, hear us.

Glory to the FATHER bring,
JESU! unto Thee we sing,
HOLY GHOST, Thy praises ring;
  Alleluia!—Amen,

216

JESU, SON of GOD Most High,
GOD from all eternity,
Born as man to live and die—
  Hear us, Holy JESU.

Leaving Thine eternal Throne,
Making mortal care Thine own,
Making GOD's compassion known—
    Hear us, Holy JESU.

Offspring of the lowly maid,
Born within the stable's shade,
In a rough, hard manger laid—
    Hear us, Holy JESU.

Borne in Joseph's trembling hand,
Worshipped by the shepherd band,
And the wise from far-off land—
    Hear us, Holy JESU.

Carried to the house of prayer,
Each appointed rite to share,
Circumcised, presented there—
    Hear us, Holy JESU.

Sought by Herod's envious might,
Into Egypt borne by night,
Angels guiding Thee in flight—
    Hear us, Holy JESU.

Taught Thy foster-father's trade,
Subject to the holy maid,
Though the GOD Whom she obeyed—
    Hear us, Holy JESU.

With an ever clearer view
Seeking what Thy Heart foreknew
Of the work Thou cam'st to do—
    Hear us, Holy JESU.

Moving onward while Thine Eye
Sees the Cross each day more nigh,
Still resolved for us to die—
    Hear us, Holy JESU.

By the Angels' holy song,
As around they wondering throng,
Owning Thee their Ruler strong—
    Hear us, Holy JESU.

By the lowly cattle shed,
By the narrow manger bed,
Where Thine Infant Form was laid—
    Hear us, Holy JESU.

By the solemn praise and prayer,
By the gifts and offerings rare
Brought in lowly homage there—
    Hear us, Holy JESU.

By Thy growing day by day,
By Thy zeal in wisdom's way,
Quick to learn and to obey—
    Hear us, Holy JESU.

By Thy life, so lone and still,
By Thy waiting to fulfil
In its time Thy FATHER's will—
    Hear us, Holy JESU.

By the care that weighed on Thee,
By Thy toil and poverty,
By Thy sorrows yet to be—
    Hear us, Holy JESU.

Make us ever long to know
Where our GOD would have us go,
Shrinking not from toil or woe—
    Hear us, Holy JESU.

May we mark the pattern fair
Of Thy life of work and prayer,
And for truth all perils dare—
    Hear us, Holy JESU.

May we calmly suffer blame,
Bear the cross, despise the shame,
In Thy strength and in Thy Name—
    Hear us, Holy JESU.

As we live from year to year,
JESU, be Thou ever near,
Make us like Thee, Saviour dear—
    Hear us, Holy JESU.

Bid us come at last, to Thee,
And for ever perfect be,
Where Thy glory we shall see—
    Hear us, Holy JESU.—Amen.

217

Day of wrath! that day of mourning!
See fulfill'd the prophets' warning,
Heaven and earth in ashes burning!

O what fear man's bosom rendeth,
When from heaven the Judge descendeth,
On Whose sentence all dependeth!

Lo! the Book exactly worded,
Wherein all hath been recorded:
Thence shall justice be awarded.

King of Majesty tremendous,
Who dost free salvation send us,
Fount of pity! then befriend us!

Think, kind JESU, my salvation
Cost Thy wondrous Incarnation:
Leave me not to reprobation!

Faint and weary, Thou hast sought me,
On the Cross of suffering bought me.
Shall such grace in vain be brought me?

Righteous Judge! for sin's pollution
Grant Thy gift of absolution,
Ere that day of retribution.

While the wicked are confounded,
Doomed to flames of woe unbounded,
Call me with Thy Saints surrounded.

Bow my heart in meek submission,
Strewn with ashes of contrition;
Help me in my lost condition.

Day of sorrows, day of weeping,
When, in dust no longer sleeping,
Man awakes in Thy dread keeping!

To the rest Thou didst prepare him
By Thy Cross, O CHRIST upbear him;
Spare, O GOD, in mercy spare him.

LORD, all-pitying, JESUS Blest,
Grant them Thine eternal rest. Amen.

218

We march, we march to victory
  With the Cross of the LORD before us,
With His loving Eye looking down from
    the sky,
  And His Holy Arm spread o'er us,
  His Holy Arm spread o'er us.

We come in the might of the LORD of
    Light
  In surpliced train to meet Him:
And we put to flight the armies of night,
  That the sons of the day may greet Him,
  The sons of the day may greet Him.

We march, we march to victory,
  With the Cross of the LORD before us,
With His loving Eye looking down
    from the sky,
  And His Holy Arm spread o'er us.

The bands of the Alien flee away
  When our chant goes up like thunder,
And the van of the LORD in serried array,
  Cleaves Satan's ranks asunder.
    We march, we march, &c.

Our sword is the Spirit of GOD on High,
  Our helmet His Salvation;
Our banner the Cross of Calvary,
  Our watchword the IN-CAR-NA-TION.
    We march, we march, &c.

He marches in front of His banner un-
    furl'd,
  Which He raised that His own might
    find Him;
And the Holy Church throughout all the
    world
  Falls into rank behind Him.
    We march, we march, &c.

And the choir of Angels with song awaits
  Our march in the golden Sion;
For our Captain has broken the brazen
    gates,
  And burst the bars of iron.
    We march, we march, &c.

Then onward we march, our arms to prove
  With the banner of CHRIST before us,
With His Eye of love looking down from
    above,
  And His Holy Arm spread o'er us.
    We march, we march, &c.

219

Faith of our Fathers! Living still
 In spite of dungeon, fire and sword,
Oh, how our hearts beat high with joy
 Whene'er we hear that glorious Word.
  Faith of our Fathers! Holy Faith!
  We will be true to thee till death.

Our Fathers, chained in prisons dark,
 Were still in heart and conscience free,
How sweet would be their children's fate,
 If they like them could die for thee.
  Faith of our Fathers! etc.

Faith of our Fathers! Faith and Prayer
 Must win our country back to thee,
And through the Truth that comes from GOD,
 This land shall then indeed be free.
  Faith of our Fathers! etc.

Faith of our Fathers! We will love
 Both friend and foe in all our strife,
And preach thee too, as love knows how,
 By kindly word and virtuous life.
  Faith of our Fathers! etc.
   —Amen.

220

GOD the FATHER, GOD the SON,
GOD the SPIRIT. THREE in ONE,
Hear us from Thy heavenly Throne,
 Spare us, Holy TRINITY.

JESU, Who for us didst bear
Scorn and sorrow, toil and care,
Hearken to our lowly prayer;
 Hear us, Holy JESU.

By that hour of Agony,
Spent while Thine Apostles three
Slumbered in Gethsemane,
    Hear us, Holy JESU.

By the prayer Thou thrice didst pray
That the cup might pass away,
So Thou mightest still obey,
    Hear us, Holy JESU.

By the kiss of treachery
To Thy foes betraying Thee,
By Thy harsh captivity,
    Hear us, Holy JESU.

By the scourging Thou hast borne,
By the purple robe of scorn,
By the reed and crown of thorn,
    Hear us, Holy JESU.

By the insult of the Jews,
When Barabbas they would choose,
And did Thee their King refuse,
    Hear us, Holy JESU.

By Thy going forth to die,
When they raised the wicked cry,
"Crucify Him, crucify!"
    Hear us, Holy JESU.

By the Cross which Thou didst bear,
By the cup they bade Thee share,
Mingled gall and vinegar,
    Hear us, Holy JESU.

By Thy nailing to the Tree,
By the title over Thee,
By the gloom of Calvary,
    Hear us, Holy JESU.

By the parting of Thy clothes,
By the mocking of Thy foes,
As they watched Thy dying woes.
    Hear us, Holy JESU.

By Thy seven Words then said,
By the bowing of Thy Head,
By Thy numbering with the dead.
    Hear us, Holy JESU.

When temptation sore is rife,
When we faint amidst the strife,
Thou, Whose death hath been our life,
    Save us, Holy JESU.

While on stormy seas we toss,
Let us count all things as loss
But Thee only on Thy Cross:
    Save us, Holy JESU.

So, with hope in Thee made fast,
When death's bitterness is past
We may see Thy Face at last:
    Hear us, Holy JESU.—Amen.

221

GOD the FATHER, GOD the Word,
GOD the HOLY GHOST adored,
Blessed TRINITY, one LORD;
    Spare us, Holy TRINITY.

JESU, for us sinners slain,
Temple, levelled to the plain,
After three days raised again.
    Hear us, Holy JESU.

JESU, Who from hell did pass,
Bursting, as they were but glass,
Iron bars, and gates of brass:
    Hear us, Holy JESU.

Jesu, bearing to Thy fold
Patriarchs and Seers of old,
Loosed for aye from that dark hold;
    Hear us, Holy Jesu.

Jesu, Whom no threefold ward—
Stone, and seal, and soldier guard—
From Thy Resurrection barred;
    Hear us, Holy Jesu.

Jesu, Whose arising glad
Angels, in white raiment clad,
Told unto the women sad;
    Hear us, Holy Jesu.

Jesu, in Thy triumph seen,
First by Mary Magdalene,
Standing where Thy grave had been;
    Hear us, Holy Jesu.

Jesu, Who didst calm the fear
Of Thine own Apostles dear,
Saying, "Peace, for I am here;"
    Hear us, Holy Jesu.

Jesu, Who didst then ascend
To the realm which hath no end,
And the Spirit down didst send,
    Hear us, Holy Jesu.

Jesu, Who thus gavest speech,
To the Twelve Thy Name to preach,
And the darkened world to teach,
    Hear us, Holy Jesu.

That we, buried in Thy grave
By the pure baptismal wave,
May there find Thee strong to save,
    We beseech Thee, Jesu.

That we rise from death of sin,
And through Thy dear grace, may win
Perfect peace our souls within,
    We beseech Thee, JESU.

That we daily live to Thee,
Striving in humility,
Godly, pure, and just to be,
    We beseech Thee, JESU.

Weaning us from earthly toys,
Grant the prize that never cloys,
Turn our sorrows into joys,
    We beseech Thee, JESU.

When hath come the day of dread,
And the graves give up their dead,
Take Thy members to their Head,
    We beseech Thee, JESU.

Grant us, when we rise again,
Purified from mortal stain,
Evermore with Thee to reign,
    We beseech Thee, JESU.—Amen.

222

GOD the FATHER, GOD the WORD,
GOD the HOLY GHOST adored,
Blessed TRINITY, one LORD,
    Spare us, Holy TRINITY.

Holy SPIRIT, wondrous Love,
Dew descending from above,
Breath of Life and GOD of Love,
    Hear us, Holy SPIRIT.

LORD of strength and knowledge clear,
Wisdom, Godliness sincere,
Understanding, Counsel, Fear,
    Hear us, Holy SPIRIT.

Giver of meekness, love and peace,
Patience, pureness, faith's increase,
Mercy, joy that cannot cease,
  Hear us, Holy SPIRIT.

Teacher of all innocence,
Goodness, virtue, temperance,
In temptation strong defence,
  Hear us, Holy SPIRIT.

Thou, Who, overshadowing
Blessed Mary with Thy wing,
Madest her to bear the King,
  Hear us, Holy SPIRIT.

Thou, Who, brooding o'er the wave,
Poured the stains of sin to lave,
Comest to the font to save,
  Hear us, Holy SPIRIT.

Thou, Whose might from heaven shed
On the Wine and on the Bread,
Bringeth to us CHRIST our Head,
  Hear us, Holy SPIRIT.

Lightener of eyes that seek,
Thou Who pleadest for the weak
With those groans no tongue may speak,
  Hear us, Holy SPIRIT.

From sin's dark and woeful night,
From the world and vain delight,
From the devil and his might,
  Save us, Holy SPIRIT.

From all pride and heresy,
From all lack of purity,
From the tempter's enmity,
  Save us, Holy SPIRIT.

Thou, with Thine own cleansing dew,
Our polluted hearts renew,
Hearken ever as we sue,
    We pray Thee, Holy SPIRIT.

Thou with Thine own union bind
Soul and body, heart and mind,
In peace with GOD and all mankind,
    We pray Thee, Holy SPIRIT.

That we never quench Thy Grace,
But at last may reach the place,
Where shines JESU's glorious Face.
    We pray Thee, Holy SPIRIT.
        —Amen.

223

GOD the FATHER, GOD the SON
GOD the SPIRIT, THREE in ONE,
Hear us from Thy heavenly Throne.
    Spare us, Holy TRINITY.

JESU, with Thy Church abide,
Be her SAVIOUR, LORD and Guide,
While on earth her faith is tried:
    We beseech Thee, hear us.

Arms of love around her throw,
Shield her safe from every foe,
Comfort her in time of woe:
    We beseech Thee, hear us.

Keep her life and doctrine pure,
Grant her patience to endure,
Trusting in Thy promise sure:
    We beseech Thee, hear us.

May her voice be ever clear;
Warning of a judgment near,
Telling of a SAVIOUR dear:
 We beseech Thee, hear us.

All her fettered powers release,
Bid her strife and envy cease,
Grant the heavenly gift of peace;
 We beseech Thee, hear us.

All that she has lost restore,
May her strength and zeal be more
Than in brightest days of yore:
 We beseech Thee, hear us.

May she guide the poor and blind,
Seek the lost until she find,
And the broken-hearted bind:
 We beseech Thee, hear us.

Save her love from growing cold,
Make her watchmen strong and bold,
Fence her round, Thy peaceful fold:
 We beseech Thee, hear us.

May her Priests Thy people feed,
Shepherds of the flock indeed,
Ready, where Thou call'st, to lead:
 We beseech Thee, hear us.

Judge her not for work undone,
Judge her not for fields unwon,
Bless her works in Thee begun:
 We beseech Thee, hear us.

May her lamp of truth be bright,
Bid her bear aloft its light
Through the realms of heathen night:
 We beseech Thee, hear us.

Arm her soldiers with the Cross,
Brave to suffer toil or loss,
Counting earthly gain but dross:
    We beseech Thee, hear us.

May she holy tirumphs win,
Overthrow the hosts of sin,
Gather all the nations in:
    We beseech Thee, hear us.

Fit her all Thy joy to share
In the home Thou dost prepare,
And be ever blessed there:
    We beseech Thee, hear us.
              —Amen.

224

Hasten the time appointed,
  By prophets long foretold,
When all shall dwell together,
  One Shepherd and one Fold,
Let every idol perish,
  To moles and bats be thrown,
And every prayer be offer'd
  To GOD in CHRIST alone,

Let Jew and Gentile meeting
  From many a distant shore,
Around one altar kneeling,
  One common LORD adore.
Let all that now divides us
  Remove and pass away,
Like shadows of the morning
  Before the blaze of day.

Let all that now unites us
  More sweet and lasting prove,
A closer bond of union,
  In a blest land of love.

Let war be learn'd no longer,
   Let strife and tumult cease,
All earth His blessed kingdom.
   The LORD and Prince of Peace.

O long-expected dawning,
   Come with thy clearing ray!
When shall the morning brighten,
   The shadows flee away?
O sweet anticipation!
   It cheers the watchers on,
To pray, and hope, and labour,
   Till the dark night be gone.
                   —Amen.

225

Praise to the Holiest in the height,
   And in the depth be praise;
In all His works most wonderful,
   Most sure in all His ways.

O loving wisdom of our GOD!
   When all was sin and shame,
A second Adam to the fight
   And to the rescue came.

O wisest love! that flesh and blood,
   Which did in Adam fail,
Should strive afresh against the foe,
   Should strive and should prevail:

And that a higher gift than grace
   Should flesh and blood refine,
GOD'S Presence and His very Self,
   And Essence all-divine.

O generous love! that He Who smote
   In Man for man the foe,
The double agony in Man
   For man should undergo;

And in the garden secretly,
  And on the Cross on high,
Should teach His brethren, and inspire
  To suffer and to die.

Praise to the Holiest in the height,
  And in the depth be praise:
In all His words most wonderful,
  Most sure in all His ways.—Amen.

226

Now thank we all our GOD,
With heart and hands and voices,
  Who wondrous things hath done,
In Whom His world rejoices;
    Who from our mother's arms
      Hath blessed us on our way
    With countless gifts of love,
      And still is ours to-day.

O may this bounteous GOD
Through all our life be near us;
  With ever joyful hearts
And blessed peace to cheer us;
    And keep us in His Grace,
      And guide us when perplexed,
    And free us from all ills
      In this world and the next.

All praise and thanks to GOD
The FATHER now be given,
  The SON, and HIM Who reigns
With Them in highest heaven,
    The ONE Eternal GOD,
      Whom earth and heaven adore,
    For thus it was, is now,
      And shall be evermore.—Amen.

227

God the Father, God the Son,
God the Spirit, Three in One,
Hear us from Thy heavenly Throne,
    Spare us, Holy Trinity.

Jesu, Life of those who die,
Advocate with God on high,
Hope of immortality,
    Hear us, Holy Jesu.

Thou Whose Death to mortals gave
Power to triumph o'er the grave,
Living now from death to save,
    Hear us, Holy Jesu.

Thou before Whose great white Throne
All our doings must be shown,
Pleading now for us Thine own,
    Hear us, Holy Jesu.

Thou Whose Death was borne that we,
From the power of Satan free,
Might not die eternally,
    Hear us, Holy Jesu.

Thou Who dost a place prepare,
That in heavenly mansions fair
Sinners may Thy glory share,
    Hear us, Holy Jesu.

Death.
We are dying day by day;
Soon from earth we pass away;
Lord of life to Thee we pray;
    Hear us, Holy Jesu.

Ere we hear the Angel's call,
And the shadows round us fall,
Be our Saviour, be our All,
    Hear us, Holy Jesu.

Wean our hearts from things below,
Make us all Thy love to know.
Guard us from our ghostly foe;
  Hear us, Holy Jesu.

Shelter us with Angel's wing,
To our souls Thy pardon bring;
So shall death have lost its sting;
  Hear us, Holy Jesu.

In the gloom Thy light provide;
Safely through the valley guide;
Thee we trust, for Thou hast died:
  Hear us, Holy Jesu.

JUDGMENT.

When Thy summons we obey
On the dreadful Judgment Day,
Let not fear our soul dismay:
  Hear us, Holy Jesu.

While the lost in terror fly,
May we see with joyful eye
Our Redemption drawing nigh:
  Hear us, Holy Jesu.

May we see Thee on Thy Throne
As the SAVIOUR we have known,
And have followed as our own:
  Hear us, Holy Jesu.

May we then, among the blest
Who Thy Name on earth confessed,
Hear Thee calling us to rest:
  Hear us, Holy Jesu.

HELL.

From the awful place of doom,
Where in rayless outer gloom
Dead souls lie as in a tomb,
  Save us, Holy Jesu.

From the black, the dull dispair
Ruined men and angels share,
From the dread companions there,
    Save us, Holy JESU.

From the unknown agonies
Of the soul that helpless lies,
From the worm that never dies,
    Save us, Holy JESU.

From the lusts that none can tame,
From the fierce mysterious flame,
From the everlasting shame,
    Save us, Holy JESU.

HEAVEN.
Where Thy Saints in glory reign,
Free from sorrow, free from pain,
Pure from every guilty stain,
    Bring us, Holy JESU.

Where the captives find release,
Where all foes from troubling cease,
Where the weary rest in peace,
    Bring us, Holy JESU.

Where the pleasures never cloy,
Where in Angels' holy joy
Thy redeemed their powers employ,
    Bring us, Holy JESU.

Where in wondrous light are shown
All Thy dealings with Thine own,
Who shall know as they are known,
    Bring us, Holy JESU.

Where, with loved ones gone before,
We may love Thee and adore
In Thy Presence evermore,
    Bring us, Holy JESU.—Amen.

228

"Stay, MASTER, stay, upon this heavenly
    hill;
A little longer let us linger still;
With these two mighty ones of old beside,
Near to the Awful Presence still abide;
Before the throne of light we trembling
    stand,
And catch a glance into the Spirit-land."

"Stay, MASTER, stay! we breathe a purer
    air;
This life is not the life that waits us there;
Thoughts, feelings, flashes, glimpses,
    come and go;
We cannot speak them—nay, we do not
    know;
Wrapt in this cloud of light, we seem to
    be
The thing we fain would grow—eter-
    nally"

"No!" saith the LORD, "the hour is past;
    we go:
Our home, our life, our duties lie below.
While here we kneel upon the mount of
    prayer,
The plough lies waiting in the furrow
    there;
Here we sought GOD that we might know
    His Will;
There we must do it—serve Him—seek
    Him still."

"If man aspires to reach the throne of
    GOD,
O'er the dull plains of earth must lie the
    road.

He who best does his lowly duty here,
Shall mount the highest in a nobler sphere:
At GOD's own feet our spirits seek their rest,
And he is nearest Him who serves Him best." —Amen.

229

JESUS! Name of wondrous love!
Name all other names above!
Unto which must every knee
Bow in deep humility.

JESUS! Name decreed of old;
To the maiden Mother told,
Kneeling in her lowly cell,
By the angel Gabriel.

JESUS! Name of priceless worth
To the fallen sons of earth,
For the promise that it gave—
"JESUS shall His people save."

JESUS! Name of mercy mild,
Given to the holy Child,
When the cup of human woe
First He tasted here below.

JESUS! Only Name that's given
Under all the mighty heaven,
Whereby man to sin enslaved,
Bursts his fetters, and is saved.

JESUS! Name of wondrous love!
Human Name of GOD above;
Pleading only this we flee,
Helpless, O our GOD, to Thee.
—Amen.

230

Come, ye thankful people, come,
Raise the song of Harvest-home:
All is safely gathered in,
Ere the winter storms begin;
God, our Maker, doth provide
For our wants to be supplied;
Come to God's own Temple, come,
Raise the song of Harvest-home.

All this world is God's own field,
Fruit unto His praise to yield;
Wheat and tares therein are sown,
Unto joy or sorrow grown;
Ripening with a wondrous power
Till the final Harvest-hour:
Grant, O Lord of life, that we
Holy grain and pure may be

For we know that Thou wilt come,
And wilt take Thy people home;
From Thy field wilt purge away
All that doth offend, that day;
And Thine Angel's charge at last
In the fire the tares to cast,
But the fruitful ears to store
In Thy garner evermore.

Come then, Lord of mercy, come,
Bid us sing Thy Harvest-home:
Let Thy saints be gathered in,
Free from sorrow, free from sin:
All upon the golden floor
Praising Thee for evermore:
Come, with all Thine Angels come;
Bid us sing Thy Harvest-home.
—Amen.

231

God, Who madest earth and heaven,
    Darkness and light;
Who the day for toil hast given,
    For rest the night;
May Thine Angel-guards defend us,
Slumber sweet Thy mercy send us,
Holy dreams and hopes attend us,
    This livelong night.

Guard us waking, guard us sleeping,
    And when we die,
May we in Thy mighty keeping
    All peaceful lie:
When the last dread call shall wake us,
Do not Thou our God forsake us,
But to reign in glory take us
    With Thee on high.—Amen.

232

Onward, brothers, onward,
    Lift on high the strain
Floating ever sun-ward
    O'er the crystal main,
Where love's endless rapture stills each earthborn sigh;
Holy, Holy, Holy, is the Lord most High.

Onward, though in sadness.
    Though the night be dark,
Though the waves in madness
    Toss around the ark:
Still above the tempest raise the victor-song;
"Glory, laud and honour to our God belong.

Onward! Still before us
    Floats the incense cloud,
God in love shines o'er us,
    Through the battle-shroud,
Who through light and shadow led His
    people's flight—
Holy, Holy, Holy—in His loving might.

Onward through the waters
    Of the rolling sea—
Israel's sons and daughters
    Evermore are free—
Through the desert chanting with the
    ransom'd throng,
"Glory, laud and honour to our God belong."

Onward still, nor weary,
    Morning is at hand,
Through the midnight dreary
    Glows the promised land,
O'er its golden valleys floats through
    endless rest,
"Holy, Holy, Holy art Thou, LORD most
    blest."

Onward! no retreating,
    Jordan rolls before,
And our Captain's greeting
    Sounds from yonder shore;
O'er its dark blue waters, comes a burst
    of song,
"Glory, laud and honour to our God belong."

Onward! where the willows
    Droop o'er Label's stream,
Onward! where the billows
    Round our pathway gleam,

Onward! lift your voices with the choirs
    above,
"Holy! Holy! Holy! is the God of
    Love."

Onward! till the morrow
    Floods with joy the skies,
And all earthly sorrow
    In its rapture dies,
"Holy! Holy! Holy!" swell the end-
    less song,
"Glory, laud and honour to our God be-
    long."   —Amen.

233

Come forth, come forth, brave reapers!
    And bear your sheaves with you,
We come to thank the Master,
    The Master good and true;
We toil and plant, we water,
    Our labours never cease,
But God alone is Master,
    Who giveth the increase.

We sow in tears and labour,
    We reap in joy and strength,
We tread our pathway weeping,
    Good seed we bear at length;
Our mouth is filled with laughter;
    Our tongue is filled with mirth,
The Harvest is of Heaven,
    The labour was of earth.

The LORD of life saith to us,
    "Come gather in your wheat?
But when you keep your harvest,
    One thing do not forget:

There comes another Harvest
   For which no mortal delves,
There I am Harvest-Master,
   The sheaves are you yourselves.—

My Angels are the Reapers,
   Both night and day they care
To see the seed grow riper
   Within the bending ear:
At last through Heaven's bright portal
   The Guardian Angels sweep,
And say, 'The corn is ready,
   Give, LORD, the word to reap.'"

And then the word is given,
   "Go forth and reap the corn,
The fields so white to Harvest,
   Upon this Harvest morn:
Go forth, My Angel Reapers,
   And in your bosoms bear
The sheaves to My full garner,
   And store the Harvest there."—Amen.

234

Hail to Thee! true Body, sprung
   From the Virgin Mary's womb!
The same that on the Cross was hung,
   And bore for man the bitter doom!
     Son of Mary, JESU blest,
     Sweetest, gentlest, holiest!

Thou Whose Side was pierced, and flowed
   Both with water and with blood;
Suffer us to taste of Thee,
   When comes our life's last agony;
     Son of Mary, JESU blest,
     Sweetest, gentlest, holiest!
                —Amen.

ALPHABETICAL INDEX.

A few more years shall roll.................. 1
A rhyme, a rhyme for Eastertime.......116
Abide with Me, fast falls the eventide......148
Above the clear blue sky....................120
All glory, laud and honour.................. 82
All hail the power of Jesus' Name..........164
All shall call thee Blessed................. 10
Alleluia ! (3)—O sons and daughters 113
Alleluia ! (3)—The strife is o'er............. 74
Alleluia, sing to Jesus..................... 11
Alleluia, song of sweetness.................133
And now, O Father, mindful of the love. ... 80
Angels from the realm of glory.............. 73
Art thou weary, Art thou languid........... 56
As we tread life's weary journey...........202
As with gladness men of old................169
At even ere the sun was set................210
At the Cross her station keeping............ 92
At the Lamb's high feast we sing...........103
At the Name of Jesus.......................200

Before the Throne of God above............ 4
Behold a humble train......................188
Behold the Lamb of God..................... 98
Beneath the Cross of Jesus................. 49
Blessed city, heavenly Salem...............213
Blessed feasts of blessed Martyrs..........185
Blest are the pure in heart................. 77
Brightest and best of the sons of the morning..127
Brightly gleams our banner.................124
Brother, now thy toils are o'er.............147

Children of the heavenly King..............139
Christ is made the sure Foundation.........214
Christ the Lord is risen to-day............178
Christ, Who once amongst us................155
Christian, dost thou see them..............184
Christian, seek not yet repose.............. 64
Come forth, come forth, brave reapers.....233
Come, Holy Ghost, our souls inspire........ 66
Come sing with holy gladness...............122
Come, Thou Almighty King...................212
Come, Thou long expected Jesus............. 75
Come unto Me, ye weary..................... 38
Come ye faithful, raise the strain......... 90
Come, ye thankful people come..............230

Daily, daily sing the praises.................. 36
Day of wrath, that day of mourning.........217
Days and moments quickly flying........... 57
Do no sinful action............................ 25
Draw nigh and take the Body of... 186

Easter flowers are blooming bright.......... 94
Eucharistic Litany....................180, 181, 182

Faith of our Fathers.........................219
Faithful Cross above all others.............. 95
Faithful Shepherd hear our cry..............181
Faithful Shepherd of Thine own.............180
Far from my heavenly home............... 89
Father of all, from land and sea............. 81
Father from Thy throne on high (Litany)...215
Fling out the banner.........................207
For all the Saints, who from their labours..131
For thee, O dear, dear country..............118
Forever with the LORD..... 63
Forth to the fight, ye ransomed............. 37
Forty days and forty nights..... 70
Forward, forward, Christians................183
From Greenland's icy Mountains...........161
From paine to paine and woe to woe........172
From the Eastern Mountains 159

Glory be to Jesus............................ 72
God the Father, God the Son (see Litanies)
God the Father, hear us (Litanies for Advent
    and Lent.]
God, Who madest earth and heaven........231
Golden harps are sounding................... 97
Good it is to keep the Fast...................196
Great God, what do I see and hear..........136
Greet the Cross with veneration.......... ...173
Hail Festal Day............................. 96
Hail the day that sees Him rise..............101
Hail the Sign................................. 18
Hail to the Lord's Anointed.................. 22
Hail to Thee, true Body sprung.............231
Hark, hark my soul, angelic songs...........193
Hark my soul it is the Lord.............. ..157
Hark, the hearald angels sing.......... .. .160
Hark the sound of holy voices................129
Hasten the time appointed...................224
Have mercy on us, God most high..........143
Hear Thy children, gentle Jesus............. 83
Holy Ghost, come down upon Thy children.114
Holy, holy, holy, Lord God Almighty........152
Holy, holy, holy, Lord, God of Hosts.......192
How sweet the Name of Jesus sounds.......158

I am a faithful Catholic	30
I heard the voice of Jesus say	40
I love the Holy Angels	198
I love to tell the Story	67
I worship Thee Lord Jesu	170
If I could be an angel	211
I'm but a stranger here	39
In His own raiment clad	104
In the hour of trial	50
In the wintry heaven	23
Jerusalem my happy home	119
Jerusalem on high	13
Jerusalem the golden	150
Jesu, gentlest Saviour	156
Jesu, in loving worship	154
Jesu, Lover of my soul	69
Jesu, meek and gentle	135
Jesu, my Lord, my God (Jesu, My Lord)	162
Jesu, my Lord, my God (Sweet Sacrament)	27
Jesu, Son of God most high (Litany)	216
Jesu, we adore Thee	149
Jesus calls us, o'er the tumult	43
Jesus Christ is risen to-day	99
Jesus, high in glory	145
Jesus, I my Cross have taken	53
Jesus, Master, King of Glory	209
Jesus, Name of wondrous love	
Jesus, the very thought of Thee	55
Jesus, we love to meet	76
Just as I am without one plea	68
Lead kindly Light	35
Lead us heavenly Father, lead us	130
Let saints on earth in concert sing	201
Let us now go to Bethlehem	168
Lift up, lift up ye heavenly gates	132
Litanies, (see Index for Seasons and Subjects.)	
Look, ye Saints, the sight is glorious	190
Lord, is this Thy mercy's day	174
Lord of our life and God of our salvation	138
Lord speak to me that I may speak	203
Love Divine, all love excelling	175
My faith looks up to Thee	42
My God, how wonderful Thou art	168
My God, my Father, while I stray	58
Nearer my God to Thee	28
Nearer my God to Thee, and versions	60
Now my tongue the mystery telling	144

Now thank we all our God 226
Now the day is over 8

O come, all ye faithful 153
O come and mourn with me awhile 86
O come, O come, Emmanuel 145
O come to the merciful Saviour 54
O day of rest and gladness 20
O happy band of pilgrims 160
O happy Fold, O happy Church 3
O Jesus, it was surely sweet 29
O Jesus Christ remember 102
O Jesus, I have promised 53
O Jesus, Thou art standing 2
O mother dear, Jerusalem 15
O sacred Head, surrounded 88
O Saving Victim, opening wide 9
O sons and daughters, let us sing 113
O Word of God above 195
O Word of God incarnate 208
O worship Jesus now 199
Of the Father's love begotten 5
Oft in danger, oft in woe 125
Oh grant to each before Thee now 166
Oh what the joy and the glory must be 128
On Jordan's bank the Baptist's cry 142
On the Resurrection morning 194
Once in Royal David's City 161
Onward! brothers onward 232
Onward, Christian soldiers 112
Our blest Redeemer, ere He breathed 115
Our Lord He was a carpenter 106

Penitential Litany 179
Pleasant are Thy courts above 121
Praise to the Holiest in the height 225

Rejoice, rejoice believers 34
Rejoice, ye pure in heart 108
Ride on, ride on in majesty 91
Rock of Ages 65

Saviour, again to Thy dear Name 171
Saviour, blessed Saviour 126
Saviour, like a Shepherd lead us 32
See, amid the winter's snow 123
See the destined day arise 85
Shall we not love thee, Mother dear 12
Shepherd, Who Thy life didst give 182
Shout the glad tidings 191
Sing Alleluia forth in duteous praise 187
Soldiers of Christ arise 78

Spouse of Christ, in arms contending........ 46
Stand up, stand up for Jesus.................. 26
Stay, Master, stay upon this hill 228
Story of the Cross 104
Sun of my soul................................146
Sweet Saviour bless us ere we go............ 79
Sweet the moments, rich in blessing......... 87

Take my life and let it be.................... 51
The Church is my Mother.....................205
The Church's One Foundation................111
The Church, the Church, the Holy Church..206
The day is past and over...................... 16
The first Nowell the Angel did say..........141
The God of Abraham praise..................189
The hours of day are over..................... 19
The King of love, my Shepherd..............107
The Royal Banners forward go..............176
The Saints all crowned with glory..........137
The Saints of God, their conflict past.......140
The snow lay on the ground.................. 24
The Son of God goes forth to war............134
The Story of the Cross........................104
The strife is o'er.............................. 74
The sun is sinking fast 33
Thee we adore, O hidden Saviour........... 45
There is a Fountain filled with Blood........ 62
There is a Fountain filled with Blood (2nd
    Version)................................. 204
There is a green hill far away................ 93
There is One true and only God..............151
There's a Friend for little children..........110
Thou art Coming, O my Saviour.............197
Three in One and One in Three.............. 6
Through the night of doubt and sorrow....109
Thy Kingdom Come, O God.................. 14
To Christ the Prince of Peace................ 44

We are but little children weak..............117
We love the place, O God.................... 31
We march, we march.........................218
Weary of earth and laden with............. 177
What a Friend we have in Jesus............. 48
What Child is this............................ 21
When God of old came down from Heaven 193
When, His Salvation bringing............... 71
When I survey the wondrous Cross.......... 41
When morning gilds the skies................ 7
When our heads are bowed with woe........ 84
Who is this, so weak and helpless............185
Work for the night is coming................ 59

INDEX FOR SEASONS AND SUBJECTS.

EVENING.

Abide with me, fast falls................	148
At even ere the sun was set.............	210
God, Who madest earth and heaven.......	231
Hear Thy children, gentle Jesus..........	83
Now the day is over.....................	8
Saviour again to Thy dear Name..........	171
Sun of my soul.........................	146
Sweet Saviour, bless us ere we go........	79
The day is past and over................	16
The hours of day are over...............	19
The sun is sinking fast..................	33

SUNDAY—THE LORD'S DAY.

Jesus, we love to meet..................	76
O day of rest and gladness...............	20

ADVENT.

A few more years shall roll..............	1
Christian, seek not yet repose...........	64
Come, Thou long-expected Jesus..........	75
Day of wrath, that day of mourning......	217
Days and moments quickly flying........	57
God the Father, hear us, (Litany)........	17
Great God, what do I see and hear.......	136
Litany, (Four Last Things)..............	227
Love Divine, all love excelling...........	175
O come, O come, Emmanuel..............	145
O Jesus, Thou art standing..............	2
On Jordan's bank, the Baptist's cry......	142
Rejoice, rejoice believers................	34
Thou art coming, O my Saviour..........	197
Thy Kingdom come, O God...............	14
Work, for the night is coming...........	59

CHRISTMAS

Angels from the realms of glory..........	74
In the wintry heaven....................	23
Jesus, Son of God most high, (Litany)....	216
Let us now go to Bethlehem..............	168
Litany—Holy Childhood.................	216
O come, all ye faithful..................	153
Of the Father's love begotten............	5
Once in the Royal David's city...........	61
Praise to the Holiest in the height.......	225
See, amid the winter's snow..............	123
Shout the glad tidings...................	191

The first Nowell the Angel did say 141
The snow lay on the ground.................. 24
What child is this.......................... 21

THE CIRCUMCISION AND HOLY NAME.

All hail the power of Jesus' Name.......... 164
At the Name of Jesus....................... 200
How sweet the Name of Jesus sounds...... 158
Jesus, Name of wondrous love.............. 229

EPIPHANY.

As with gladness men of old................. 169
Brightest and best of the sons of............ 127
From the Eastern mountains............... 159
In the wintry heaven....................... 28
Saviour, blessed Saviour................... 126

THE WEEK BEFORE SEPTUAGESIMA.

Alleluia, song of sweetness................. 133

LENT.

A few more years shall roll.................   1
Art thou weary, art thou languid............ 56
As we tread life's weary journey............ 202
Beneath the Cross of Jesus................. 49
Christian, dost thou see them............... 184
Christian, seek not yet repose.............. 64
Come unto Me, ye weary.................... 38
Days and moments quickly flying............ 57
Forth to the fight, ye ransomed............. 37
Forty days and forty nights................. 70
From pain to pain and woe to woe.......... 172
Glory be to Jesus........................... 72
God the Father, God the Son (Litany)..... 179
God the Father, hear us (Litany)............ 47
Good it is to keep the fast.................. 196
Greet the Cross with veneration............ 173
Hail the Sign............................... 18
Hark, my soul, it is the Lord............... 157
Have Mercy on us, God most high.......... 143
I heard the voice of Jesus say.............. 40
I love to tell the story..................... 67
I'm but a stranger here.................... 39
In the hour of trial........................ 50
Jesu, Lover of my soul..................... 69
Jesu, meek and gentle...................... 135
Jesus calls us o'er the tumult.............. 43
Jesus, I my cross have taken............... 52
Jesus Master King of glory................. 209
Jesus, the very thought of Thee............ 55
Just as I am, without one plea............. 68

Litanies, (see Index for Seasons and Subjects.)
Lord, in this, Thy mercy's day..............174
My faith looks up to Thee.................... 42
My God, my Father, while I stray.......... 58
Nearer, my God, to Thee............. 28
Nearer, my God, to Thee (2nd version)....... 60
O come to the merciful Saviour.............. 54
O happy band of pilgrims..... 160
O Jesus I have promised..................... 53
Oft in danger, oft in woe.................... 125
Penitential Litany...........................179
Rock of Ages................................. 65
Soldiers of Christ, arise... 78
Stand up, stand up for Jesus................. 26
Story of the Cross...........................104
Take my life and let it be.................... 51
There is a fountain filled with Blood........ 62
There is a fountain filled with Blood (2nd Version)...................................204
There is a green hill... 93
To Christ the Prince of Peace............. .. 44
Weary of earth, and laden with..............177
What a Friend we have in Jesus............. 48
When I survey the wondrous Cross........ 41
Who is this, so weak and helpless.... 100
Work for the night is coming............. .. 59

PASSION SUNDAY (5TH LENT).
The Royal Banners forward go......... 176

PALM SUNDAY. (S. BEFORE EASTER.)
All glory, laud and honour................... 82
Ride on, ride on in majesty..... 91
When His salvation bringing................. 71

THE CROSS AND PASSION.
Art thou weary, art thou languid............ 56
As we tread life's weary journey....... ..,. 202
At the Cross her station keeping............ 92
Beneath the Cross of Jesus.................. 49
Faithful Cross above all others.............. 95
Fling out the banner........................207
Glory be to Jesus........ 72
Greet the Cross with veneration,........ 173
Hail the Sign................................ 18
Jesus, I my Cross have taken................ 52
Jesus Master, King of Glory.... 209
Litany of Passion...........................220
O come and mourn with me awhile........... 86
O sacred Head, surrounded................... 88

Rock of Ages	65
See the destined day arise	88
Sweet the moments, rich in blessing	87
The Royal Banners forward go	176
There is a Fountain filled with Blood	62
There is a Fountain filled with Blood (2nd version.)	204
There is a green hill far away	93
To Christ the Prince of Peace	44
When I survey the wondrous Cross	41
When our heads are bowed with woe	84

EASTER.

A rhyme, a rhyme for Easter time	116
At the Lamb's high Feast we sing	103
Christ the Lord is risen to-day	178
Come, ye faithful, raise the strain	90
Easter flowers are blooming bright	94
Hail Festal Day	96
Jesus Christ is risen to-day, Alleluia	99
Litany of Resurection	221
O sons and daughters let us sing	113
On the Resurrection morning	194
The strife is o'er	74

ROGATION DAYS.

Father of all, from land and sea	81
Lord of our life, and God of our salvation	138

ASCENSION.

All hail the power of Jesus Name	164
Alleluia, sing to Jesus	11
At the Name of Jesus	200
Golden harps are sounding	97
Hail the day that sees Him rise	101
Jesus, high in glory	145
Look ye saints the sight is glorious	190
The King of Love my Shepherd is	107

WHITSUN-TIDE.

Come Holy Ghost, our souls inspire	66
Holy Ghost, come dawn upon Thy children	114
Litany of the Holy Spirit	222
Our blest Redeemer ere He breathed	115
When God of old came down	193

THE CHURCH.

Faith of our Fathers	219
Forth to the fight, ye ransomed	37
Forward, forward, Christians	183
Let Saints on earth in concert sing	201
Litany of the Church	223

O happy Fold, O happy Church............. 3
Onward, Christian soldiers..... 112
Pleasant are Thy courts above...............121
Spouse of Christ, in arms contending........ 46
The Church's one Foundation................111
The Church is my mother....................205
The Church, the Church, the Holy Church .206
Through the night of doubt and sorrow.....109
We love the place, O God..................... 31

THE HOLY SCRIPTURES.
O word of God Incarnate....................208

TRINITY,
Faith of our Fathers..........................219
Have mercy on us, God most high............143
Holy, holy, holy, Lord God Almighty.......152
Holy, holy, holy, Lord God of hosts.........192
There is One True and Only God............151
Three in One, and One in Three............. 6

HOLY EUCHARIST.
Draw nigh and take 186
Now my tongue the mystery telling.........144
Thou art coming, O my Saviour.. 197
AFTER CONSECRATION.
Alleluia, sing to Jesus....................... 11
And now, O Father mindful of the love.... 80
Behold, the Lamb of God.................... 98
Hail to Thee, true Body sprung............. 234
I worship Thee, Lord Jesus..................170
Jesu, in loving worship......................154
Jesu Lover of my soul.................. 69
Jesu, meek and gentle........... 135
Jesu, my Lord, my God (Jesu my Lord)......162
Jesu, my Lord, my God Sweet (Sacrament).. 27
Jesu, we adore Thee.........................149
Jesus, the very thought of Thee............. 55
Just as I am, without one plea............... 68
O Jesu, it was surely sweet................... 29
O Jesus Christ, remember....................102
O Jesus Thou art standing................... 2
O Saving Victim, opening wide............. 9
O Worship Jesus now.... 199
Saviour, blessed Saviour.................... ...126
Saviour, like a Shepherd lead us............. 32
Thee we adore, O hidden Saviour............ 45
PROCESSIONAL (returning)
Jesu, gentlest Saviour................. 156
O Jesus, I have promised................. 53
Oft in danger, oft in woe....................125

Soldiers of Christ arise........................ 78
The King of Love, my Shepherd is...........107
We love the place O God..................... 31

HARVEST AND THANKSGIVING.

Come forth, come forth, brave reapers.......233
Come, ye thankful people come..............230
Now thank we all our God....................226
Onward, brothers onward...................232

PARISH FESTIVAL.

Blessed city, heavenly Salem..................213
Christ is made the sure Foundation..........214
Now thank we all our God....................226
O Word of God above.........................195

MISSIONARY SERVICES.

Father of all from land and sea............... 81
Fling out the banner..........................207
Father of all from land and sea............... 81
Fling out the banner.........................207
From Greenland's icy mountains............. 161
Hasten the time appointed................... 224
Jesus calls us o'er the tumult................. 43
Lord speak to me that I may speak........... 203
Thy Kingdom come, O God.................. 14

GUILD SERVICES.

Do no sinful action............................ 25
Forth to the fight ye ransomed............... 37
Hail the Sign.......... 18
Oh grant to each before Thee now.......... 166
Our Lord, He was a carpenter................ 106
Spouse of Christ in arms contending.......... 46
Through the night of doubt and sorrow...... 109
Thy Kingdom come, O God.................. 14
Work, for the night is coming 59

PROCESSIONAL—(GENERAL.)

Above the clear blue sky..................... 120
At the name of Jesus......................... 200
Brightly gleams our banner................... 124
Children of the Heavenly King................ 189
Come, sing with holy gladness................ 122
Come Thou Almighty King 212
Daily, daily, sing the praises................... 36
Fling out the banner. 207
Forward, forward, Christians................. 183
Jerusalem on high............................ 13
Jerusalem the golden......................... 150
Jesus, Master, King of Glory..... 209
Lead us heavenly Father, lead us............. 130
Love divine, all love excelling................. 175

O day of rest and gladness	20
O happy band of pilgrims	160
O Mother dear, Jerusalem	15
Oft in danger, oft in woe	125
Onward, Christian soldiers	112
Onward brothers, onward	
Pleasant are Thy courts above	121
Saviour blessed Saviour	126
Stand up, stand up for Jesus	26
The Church's one foundation	111
The God of Abraham praise	189
The King of Love my Shepherd is	107
Three in One and One in Three	6
Through the night of doubt and sorrow	109
Thy Kingdom come, O God	14
We love the place, O God	31
We march, we march	218
When morning gilds the skies	7

BURIAL OF THE DEAD.

Brother, now thy toils are o'er	147
Day of wrath, that day of mourning	217
Great God, what do I see and hear	136
In the hour of trial	50
Jesu, Lover of my soul	69
My faith looks up to Thee	42
My God, my Father while I stray	59
Nearer my God to Thee	28, 60
Rock of Ages	65
There's a Friend for little children	110
When our heads are bowed with woe	84

See also the following.

HEAVEN AND FUTURE LIFE.

Daily, daily, sing the praises	36
For thee, O dear country	118
Forever with the Lord	63
Hark, hark, my soul, angelic songs	163
Hark, the sound of holy voices	129
I'm but a stranger here	39
Jerusalem my happy home	119
Jerusalem on high	13
Jerusalem the golden	150
O Mother dear, Jerusalem	15
Oh what the joy and the glory must be	198
Pleasant are Thy courts above	121
There's a Friend for little children	110

FEAST OF THE TRANSFIGURATION.

Stay, Master, stay upon this hill	228

FEASTS OF B. V. MARY.

All shall call thee Blessed	10
Behold a humble train (Purif'n)	98
Blest are the pure in heart	77
Lift up, lift up, ye heavenly gates, (Purif'n)	132
Oh grant to each before Thee now	166
Rejoice, ye pure in heart	108
Shall we not love thee Mother dear	12

THE SAINTS.

Blessed feasts of blessed martyrs	185
Daily, daily sing the praises	86
For all the Saints who from	131
Hark, the sound of holy voices	129
Jerusalem, my happy home	119
Jerusalem, on high	13
Jerusalem, the golden	150
Let Saints on earth in concert sing	201
O Mother dear, Jerusalem	15
Oh, what the joy and the glory	128
Our Lord, He was a carpenter	106
Pleasant are thy courts above	121
Sing Alleluia forth in dutious praise	187
Spouse of Christ in arms contending	46
The Saints all crowned with glory	137
The Saints of God! Their conflict past	140
The Son of God goes forth to war	134

THE ANGELS.

If I could be an Angel	211
I love the holy Angels	198

LITANIES.

Advent	17
Children's	215
Church	223
Four last things, (Advent)	227
Holy Childhood	216
Holy Eucharist	180. 181. 182
Holy Spirit	222
Lent	47
Passion	220
Penitential	179
Resurrection	221

Jesu, Name all names above
   Jesu, best and dearest,
Jesu, fount of perfect love,
   Holiest, tenderest, nearest;
Jesu, source of grace completest,
Jesu purest, Jesu sweetest,
   Jesu, well of power divine,
   Make me, keep me, seal me Thine!

Jesu, open me the gate
   That of old he enter'd,
Who, in that most lost estate,
   Wholly on Thee ventur'd;
Thou, Whose wounds are ever pleading,
And Thy Passion interceding,
   From my misery let me rise
   To a home in Paradise!

Thou didst call the prodigal:
   Thou didst pardon Mary:
Thou Whose words can never fall,
   Love can never vary:
Lord, to heal my lost condition
Give—for Thou canst give—contrition;
   Thou canst pardon all my ill
   If Thou wilt: O say, "I will!"

Woe, that I have turned aside
   After fleshly pleasure!
Woe, that I have never tried
   For the heavenly treasure!
Treasure, safe in home supernal;
Incorruptible, eternal!
   Treasure no less price hath won
   Than the Passion of the Son!

[OVER]

Jesu, crown'd with thorns for me,
   Scourged for my transgression,
Witnessing, through agony,
   That Thy good confession!
Jesu, clad in purple raiment,
For my evils making payment;
   Let not all Thy woe and pain,
   Let not Calvary be in vain!

When I reach death's bitter sea,
   And its waves roll higher,
Help the more forsaking me
   As the storm draws nigher:
Jesu, leave me not to languish,
Helpless, hopeless, full of anguish!
   Tell me—"Verily I say,
   Thou shalt be with Me to-day!"

www.ingramcontent.com/pod-product-compliance
Lightning Source LLC
Chambersburg PA
CBHW032118230426
43672CB00009B/1773